THEY DON'T LIKE ME

Ps.41

Also by Jane Katch:

*Under Deadman's Skin: Discovering the Meaning
of Children's Violent Play*

THEY DON'T LIKE ME

··

*Lessons on Bullying
and Teasing from
a Preschool Classroom*

Jane Katch

BEACON
I50

Beacon Press   BOSTON

Beacon Press
25 Beacon Street
Boston, Massachusetts 02108-2892
www.beacon.org

Beacon Press books
are published under the auspices of
the Unitarian Universalist Association of Congregations.

08 07 06 05 04   8 7 6 5 4 3 2 1

This book is printed on acid-free paper that meets the uncoated paper
ANSI/NISO specifications for permanence as revised in 1992.

The names of students in this book have been changed, as have identifying
details, to protect the privacy of the individuals involved. In addition, some
of the characters are based on composites of more than one child.

Text design by Bob Overholtzer
Composition by Wilsted & Taylor Publishing Services

Library of Congress Cataloging-in-Publication Data
Katch, Jane.
    They don't like me : lessons on bullying and teasing from a preschool
classroom / Jane Katch.
        p.   cm.
    ISBN 0-8070-2320-5 (cloth)
    ISBN 0-8070-2321-3 (paperback)
    1. Bullying in schools. 2. Discipline of children. 3. Education, Preschool.
I. Title.
    LB3013.3.K37 2003
    371.5'8—dc21

                                                                2003010498

For
   Jed
      Margaret and Hannah

Contents

1
....

Complicated

"We don't like you."

Hearing those harsh words, I look up quickly from the art table, where I am mixing the morning's paints. It is only the first week of school but I know they come from five-year-old Toby, already the vortex of conflict in my class.

From other children I may hear, "I won't invite you to my birthday party," or "You're not my friend," pronouncements intended to persuade another child to play a game or give up a toy. But Toby's statement has a more deadly message: *you have already been rejected by the group of important people in this classroom.*

In my first years of teaching, I ignored such statements, fearing that if I paid attention to them I would make the ostracized child even more uncomfortable. In the next years, I lectured the children about the importance of kindness and inclusion. But now I feel a need to understand: why does a young child, just becoming aware of the existence of the group, feel such a strong need to keep another child out?

"Let's go smash his guy," Toby tells Sean and Russell, who are sitting near him at the table, as Toby hits four-year-old Noah's small plastic truck driver with his own.

Noah slowly stands up and walks silently to the block area, his shoulders slumped and his face impassive. Rejection by his favorite group of older boys can drive him away, even from the red, blue, and yellow blocks with wheels that attach with a black screwdriver.

"What's wrong?" I ask the three boys who are sitting around the sides of the table. They avoid my eyes and my question. I look at the empty chair and then at Noah.

"They don't like me," he whispers.

"Toby's being mean to him," Sean says at last, chewing on the cuff of his red long-sleeved T-shirt.

"Why did you say, 'We don't like you'?" I ask Toby, who pushes the wisps of dark hair away from his face. Toby has a big boy's haircut, professionally trimmed along the sides and back. Noah, in contrast, still has the unruly, honey-brown curls of a younger boy. They stare at me blankly.

"Share the toys," Timmy, the youngest child in my class, suggests, remembering that adults usually approve of this solution to conflict.

"Come back here a moment, Noah," I say. He returns slowly, not knowing what I might have in mind. I hand each boy one of the plastic truck drivers. "Show me what happened in your game," I tell them. "Pretend you're playing it again."

After a pause, Toby begins. "I want to get some more power," he says, speaking for his girl truck driver.

Toby always wants more. He wants the tallest block house for his stuffed animals, the steepest incline for his car track, and the longest tail on his dragon painting. Often he's so preoccupied with getting the most, he doesn't get around to playing before it's time to clean up and have a snack.

"She's the boss bad guy," he explains now, handing her to Russell, who is sitting across the table. Russell has gel keeping the front of his red hair in a flip, just like his older brother, who walked him into the room this morning. Russell accepts the figure and puts her in a small plastic box that once held the treasure for a toy pirate set. "This is taking all of her power!" he says excitedly, as he takes the girl out of the box. Taking power from the boss bad girl seems to please all four boys and is clearly not the source of the conflict.

"What happened next?" I ask.

Noah puts his truck driver in front of him on the table. "I just put this down for a minute," he says softly.

Toby picks it up quickly, puts it in the treasure box, and closes the lid. "I took up your energy," Toby tells the figure when he opens the box. "Now you can't move."

"You can't! You can't!" Noah protests quietly, his large dark eyes looking worried.

"That sucks up power!" Toby explains to him. "This is a *real* game," he says, adding legitimacy to his argument. I am not sure where the original real game ends and the reenactment begins, but I think that if I am patient we may soon find out what led to Toby's rejection of Noah.

"You can't suck up my power!" Noah tells him earnestly. "Because this is an ice thing." He puts one finger on a small red block. "When I push this switch, there it goes! I turned into ice *before* you sucked up my energy."

I am impressed with Noah's new invention, designed on the spot to block Toby's power. But Toby is not pleased.

"No! You don't have ice power now!" Toby argues. He is in the game, forgetting this is a reenactment.

"Yeah!" Russell agrees.

Toby stops abruptly and looks at me.

"That's when he said we don't like him," Sean explains, examining the dark, wet spot he's been chewing at the end of his sleeve.

These four words threaten to suck my power, too, bringing back a string of memories beginning in kindergarten. I was the youngest in my class when the teacher said, "Put your chair in a circle." I took the command literally, searching all over the floor for a circle in which to place my chair, puzzled that all the other children seemed to know where to go. In fourth grade, the girls in the popular group all held hands in a line at recess while I wondered how they came to be the chosen ones. By sixth grade, I knew enough to pretend to have a crush on one of the boys, just to sound like the other girls, who already had the beginnings of breasts and changing hormones. I still dream that I am at a cocktail party, finally looking great in a slinky black dress, only to look down and realize I am wearing the red tie shoes of my childhood, caught again in the act of pretending to belong.

I want my classroom to be a respite, a place of safety. But more than that, I want each child to have the opportunity to belong, to learn to be a valued member of the group.

I would like to help Noah find the place he wants among these older boys. But I also know I must not alienate them during these important first weeks of school. My fours seem so innocent; they just want a good toy, preferably one with wheels, and plenty of time to explore with it. These fives, who have already told us they are six, are involved in a separate drama of power and status. They have older brothers and sisters, and they know how real big kids talk.

Noah is the bridge between these two groups. Unlike Timmy, he is no longer satisfied with just his favorite toy. Having become aware that there is a social group, he wants, more than anything, to be accepted by it. He is willing to argue the relative merits of ice power and energy-sucking machines, but Toby's words, "We don't like you," rejection in the name of the group, make him give up and walk away.

"This is complicated," I say, "and I want to understand it. Toby, are you angry because you took the energy from Noah's guy first, before he tried to stop you with his ice power?"

"That's when we said, 'We don't like you.'" Toby agrees. "He wasn't playing by the rules."

"Compel-cated, compel-cated," Russell sings softly in the background, enjoying the sound of my long word.

Now that I understand the annoyance of the older boys toward the younger child who was not following the conventions of their game, I feel more sympathetic to them. But how was it decided that Noah's figure was the one to lose power? And must he agree or leave?

"When someone plays in a way that you think is unfair, what can you do?" I ask.

Brooke and Gwynn have been listening from the art table nearby.

"Don't say, 'I don't like you,' " Brooke tells them. "That's not a nice word to say because it hurts their feelings."

"Did that hurt your feelings?" I ask Noah. He nods, his eyes large and solemn.

"You can't say, 'You can't play,' " Brooke reminds Toby. This is a rule in our school, which we adopted after the teachers read Vivian Paley's book by that name. We agreed with Paley that we wanted our young children to learn social skills by being included in the group. When a young child is rejected year after year, he or she does not have the opportunity to develop and practice the ability to become a constructive group member, an important foundation of learning at our school. I introduce the rule the first week of September and we discuss the ramifications all year.

"You can say, 'That's not fair,' " Brooke prompts Noah.

"Or, 'That's not fun,' " Gwynn adds.

"Or, 'That's not good.' "

"Or, 'That's not nice.' " The children like the rhythm of Brooke's words.

"Then you'd be bossy," Toby objects.

"If you say, 'please,' that wouldn't be bossy," Gwynn tells him.

"Let's notice when telling someone how you feel seems bossy and when it helps the problem," I say. "We'll talk about this again."

"Compel-cated, compel-cated," Russell whispers in the background.

2

....

Who Cares?

A few days later, I am sitting at our small round table writing down a story that Gwynn is dictating to me and simultaneously keeping an eye on Toby and Sean at the sand table a few feet away.

Since our discussion about the truck driver game, I have been increasingly aware of my tendency to blame Toby even before I hear his point of view, and at the same time I have become more willing to believe that his ideas about a conflict might help in its resolution. Perhaps, I muse as Gwynn pauses in her narrative, this process of listening to each other could help Toby, Sean, and Russell to have more compassion for the younger children in the class.

Still, trouble between these boys can erupt quickly, and I like to be close by. So, when I hear Toby demand, "I need a house for my animals," I pay attention.

Toby spills the toys from a small plastic container into a corner of the sand and puts the box upside down in front of him.

"Can I have that, too?" Sean asks, putting his lion cub inside it.

"I already thought of it," Toby says, pushing Sean's hand and cub aside as he asserts his ownership of both the idea and the box. There is a brief tussle and before I can put down my pen and move to the sand table, Toby screams. "He bit me! Right here!" He pushes up his sleeve and shows me his arm.

I examine the site of the injury. "There's no mark," I say. "That's good." I am looking for opportunities to help the children talk about their feelings, but I prefer to do it without having to involve the school nurse, who is then required to write a report home. "What happened, Sean?"

"He wasn't sharing!" Sean says.

"Well, I thought of it!" Toby repeats.

They both reach for the box, which I pick up and put out of reach. "I'll hold this for a minute, so no one gets hurt," I tell them. "Sean, you know that it's not OK to bite. Now can you tell Toby in words what made you so angry?"

"I'm sorry," Sean says, giving me the line he expects will appease me but looking more angry than apologetic.

"I understand that," I say, "but can you tell him what you were so angry about?"

"Toby wouldn't let us put our animals in the house," Sean says.

"Because I thought of it!" Toby says again.

"I think he should share the house," Brooke comments from the art table, where she is making a bed for her Beanie Baby puppy.

"What if we come in but we have to ask?" Sean suggests. This is a breakthrough in this impasse—a new solution to the problem.

"Maybe," Toby says.

"Toby," I say, adding my weight to Sean's proposal. "Would it be OK if they come in, if they ask you first? And if Sean will agree not to bite anymore?" I look at Sean, who nods silent agreement.

"Maybe, I said!"

"We need to make a plan before I give the box back," I say, keeping up the pressure.

"OK," Toby says, "but first we have to put some sand here, around the box." Toby keeps control of the project even as he agrees to share the animal house.

I return the box and they all get to work moving the sand and setting up their animals. I compare the quick physical aggression of the boys with the tidy verbal responses of the girls. Phrases such as "That's not a nice word" and "He should share" avoid physical confrontation, but I wonder if they might also prevent the deeper understanding of another person's point of view that could lead, eventually, to greater compassion.

"Sean said 'Who cares?' to me," Russell complains a few days later, as the two boys play with the Legos.

"Well, I *don't* care about that!" Sean answers.

"It makes me feel bad," Russell says.

"What would you like him to say instead?" I ask, trying to figure out what Russell is upset about.

"Say, 'That's a neat tail!' " Russell says.

"I didn't say, 'Who cares,' " Sean argues.

"Yeah, he did," Russell insists, looking at me. "I said, 'Sean, look how long my dragon's tail is,' and he said, 'Who cares?' And that's not saying *not* who cares!"

"Sean," I say, still puzzled, "are you angry that Russell's dragon tail is too long?" I inspect Sean's plastic dragon that seems to have a short tree sticking out from its back and then look at Russell's, which has a long gray piece attached to its rear flank.

"I couldn't find any pieces that were just as long as Sean's," Russell complains. "He said he would have a regala tail and those spiky things are not making it a regala tail! So I had to add this gray piece on mine."

"What's a regular tail?" I ask.

"It's a plain old tail," Russell says, "with nothing on it."

I begin to understand. After agreeing their dragons would have similar tails, Sean added the green tree. Russell, wanting to make sure his dragon was equally powerful, added the longer gray piece. Sean then thought Russell's was too long, and refused to admire it.

"Did you want to have the same kinds of tails?" I ask them.

"And the same length," Russell agrees, "but he doesn't want the same length."

"Sean," I ask, "would you feel OK if you had the same kind of tails, so nobody felt bad? If Russell made his tail shorter, would you take the green piece off yours?"

Sean nods agreement and puts the tree back in the box.

"Yours has to be just a little bit bigger," Russell says, putting the dragons side by side and comparing tails. The boys search happily for matching pieces, measuring and comparing until they are both satisfied.

For the moment, I am satisfied, too, that they are learning the language they need to explain their wish to compete and to find solutions to my demand that they compromise.

3

....

The Mystery of the
Dead Unicorns, Chapter 1

Zoë, a new girl, joins our class the following week. She spends the morning playing alone at the dollhouse, speaking quietly in different voices for each member of the family and showing no sign of interest in the other children.

But during recess, Michelle, one of my younger four-year-olds, comes running toward me, her blonde ponytails flying out behind her. "Zoë kicked me!" she says. "She's been on the tire swing since recess started and I told her I wanted a turn and that's when she kicked me!"

"Zoë doesn't know how we share the tire swing," I tell Michelle. "Maybe you could explain how we take turns."

Michelle and I walk over to the swing. "What happened?" I ask Zoë. She is a full year older than Michelle, but I know it is hard to be the new girl in this class that has already been together for the important first weeks of school and I want to give her the benefit of the doubt.

"She told me I had to get off!" Zoë says indignantly, flipping her tight brown braids behind her shoulders.

"You only get ten pushes," Michelle explains. "Then it's my turn."

"If someone upsets you," I tell Zoë, "there's always a teacher to help. Hitting and kicking are not allowed," I add more sternly.

I stay to watch the counting of pushes and the changing of

turns. When Zoë gets off, Michelle clambers up, tossing her a look of triumph as she passes.

"She's putting her nose in the air," Zoë tells me as we walk away. "She's vain—that's not nice."

After recess, during cleanup time, Zoë has her second interaction. While the other children are putting the blocks in matching rows on the shelf, Zoë continues her dollhouse play.

"It's cleanup time," Brooke tells her. "You have to stop playing."

Zoë turns and gives Brooke a hard shove, making her stumble against the table. "She's making announcements!" Zoë shouts. "I don't like announcements!"

I check to make sure Brooke is not hurt and talk again with Zoë about using words, not force. It's unusual for a new child to be so aggressive, and I'm beginning to worry. I hope Zoë's behavior is just a reaction to being the new girl and is not an indication of a bigger problem.

"It is time to clean up," I tell her. "See how the other children are putting the blocks away?" I decide to give her an easy way out. "Your job can be to clean up the dollhouse. Pretend that company is coming and you want the house to look beautiful." She picks up a doll from the floor and puts it on a bed inside the house. I accept that as agreement.

Each morning the children tell me stories and I write them down. We act the stories out after we clean up, with the author choosing his or her favorite role and other children taking the remaining parts. This morning, Timmy, the youngest child, has told his very first story and is eager to act it out. As we sit around the outside of the round rug, I read his one-line story:

"I drive the Power Ranger ship."

Timmy comes into the center, holds an imaginary steering wheel and drives slowly around the circle, smiling proudly. "That's the end," I say, and he returns to his seat.

"That's a short story," Gwynn comments.

"Stories can be long or short," I point out.

Nell's story is next:

"I'm a cat," she explains. "There are four cats and four dogs." I give out roles to seven children sitting around the rug. "It starts happy," I read from the notebook in which I write down Nell's stories. "At the end it's still happy." The dogs and cats smile obligingly. "First, the dogs, they run around in the yard. And the cats hide from them. And they sneak out." The eight happy pets run, sneak, and then return to their seats. Nell's story reminds me of her: she appears cheerful all day long, but is especially happy at recess, when she loves a brisk game of chase.

Toby's story is called "Are You Afraid of the Dark?" There are five good guys and three bad guys. After Gwynn chooses to be one of the good guys, Zoë decides to join her. I read:

"There's these guys that can disappear and they have sharp teeth when they get mad. And they can kill people when they get worser. And when they get to this hall with the discs it makes the creepy guys badder. And the good guys kill the bad guys."

"I want to tell a story!" Zoë demands, after the good guys have vanquished the three bad guys. Normally, I would tell her she could have a turn tomorrow, during playtime. But it seems important to help her to make positive connections with the other children to balance the negative interactions she has already created. Besides, I'm eager to hear her story. Each child's characters and plots have the potential to change the direction of the group's fantasies, and I never know what ideas will catch on and spread through the room, growing and flourishing as they expand.

So, during lunch, I sit down next to her and write her name on the front of a new notebook. "This is for all the stories you tell this year," I explain.

"I'm a fairy princess," she begins immediately. I wonder whether she always has a story in her head or whether she's been planning this one since she saw the story acting this morning. "And then I'm supposed to be flying away." She stands up beside me and starts to jump up and down with excitement. "And then I told the centaur that I just saw a dead unicorn and the centaur said, 'I think I see something over there!' "

I'm delighted with her unusual characters and exciting story line, but I interrupt her. "You can go down to the bottom of the page today," I say as I point out that we have only one line until I reach the end. "Then tomorrow you can tell a new story. That way I have enough time for everyone who wants a turn." I brace myself for a potentially explosive response from this extraordinary storyteller who does not like announcements.

"That's just chapter one," Zoë answers. "It's called 'The Mystery of the Dead Unicorns.' "

I want to end Zoë's first day on a positive note, so I decide we will act out her story before going home. Gwynn is the centaur, while Timmy cheerfully lies down to be the dead unicorn. As their conversation ends and the actors sit down, Gwynn exclaims, "That's a good story!"

"Yeah!" several children agree.

Zoë beams. "I'm telling chapter two tomorrow," she announces.

The children welcome the excitement of Zoë's story as much as I do. But will this rich fantasy life be enough to allow her to be accepted by these girls who like rules to be followed and who prefer to solve problems by taking turns rather than by force?

4
....

Are You Afraid of the Dark?

"It's so scary, know why?" Toby says to Russell and Sean at the Lego table one morning. "Once you put these little pieces on him, he gets worser and worser! He gets so worse!"

"Are you afraid of the dark?" Russell sings quietly to himself. "Gray magic is the best magic," he announces. "'Cause it can blend into anything." He snaps a long, gray cylindrical piece on his plastic figure.

"I know," Toby agrees. "It's awesome. I love when that guy fights. I need another guy," he says, picking up a detached head. He pretends the head is talking. "I need a body," he says, laughing as the head does a short, macabre dance.

"Are you afraid of the dark?" Russell sings again.

Sean turns to Noah, who is playing quietly at the other end of the table. "Noah, can you tell me what you're afraid of?" Sean asks him.

Noah looks up quickly from the spaceship he is building, pleased to have the attention of his favorite older boy. "The only thing I'm scared of is sharks," he answers.

"Ha, ha, ha, ha!" Sean laughs. "He's scared of sharks!" he announces to Toby and Russell. "We're not scared of killer whales! We're not even scared of sharks!"

I think of my favorite Calvin and Hobbes cartoon, in which six-year-old Calvin and his stuffed tiger, Hobbes, are waiting at night for the monsters to come out from under the bed. I wonder why

Toby, Sean, and Russell have to pretend they don't have such universal fears.

"We're not scared of anything!" Toby adds.

I watch Noah's face go blank as he realizes he has made a big mistake.

"That sounds unkind," I say, jumping in to defend him, "to ask him what he's scared of and then to laugh at him. I wouldn't like it if someone did that to me. Besides, it's a good thing to be afraid of something dangerous." I hear myself going on too long but can't seem to stop. "If you saw a shark in the ocean, you'd know to get out of the water." I look at Noah's serious face. "But fortunately," I add quickly, "there are hardly ever sharks around here."

"There's a shark in the pond near my house," Russell says.

"No," I tell him firmly. "You can just pretend there are sharks in the pond." I am angry with the three boys for abusing Noah's trust.

"Once I really saw a shark," Russell insists. "It wasn't in a regala pond. It was in the river."

"No," I say again. "Sharks live only in the ocean."

At our morning meeting, I return to the subject and read a book about an easily frightened lion cub who ends up rescuing his daredevil brother. I want Noah to feel all right about admitting his fear of sharks.

"It's important to respect what each person is afraid of," I tell the children when I finish reading the story. I decide not to mention the earlier incident.

"I'm scared of devils," Gwynn says immediately. "My mom told me a devil wanted to do something bad so God kicked him out of heaven."

"Devils are very bad," Toby agrees. He doesn't admit he's scared of them, I notice, but he doesn't put her down for saying so. Maybe he finds it acceptable for girls to be afraid.

"I'm scared of aliens," Timmy says.

"I'm scared of monsters," Michelle says, "'cause I have bad dreams."

"I'm scared of awnings," Noah says, so quietly that I can hardly hear.

"Awnings?" I ask, thinking I've misunderstood.

"Awnings. What you put on your house that makes it dark, so the sun doesn't get in," he explains.

"I'm not afraid of anything!" Russell says. I notice this comment follows Noah's new admission of vulnerability.

"I'm a little scared of puppies," four-year-old Nell says. "One grabbed my pants and pulled them down. And I'm scared of big dogs, 'cause one licked my mouth."

"Ew!" several children agree.

I remember Nell's story of the happy dogs and cats and wonder if successfully hiding from the dogs in fantasy is one way she masters her fears.

"And sharp teeth," Nell continues, "'cause I dream of dinosaurs with sharp teeth."

"I'm scared of roaring," Zoë says, speaking for the first time.

"Like, 'Rrrr'?" Sean asks, baring his teeth in her direction.

Nervous about Zoë's reaction, I interrupt him quickly. "If you know someone is afraid of something," I tell him, "it's important not to scare that person about it."

Have I made a mistake by encouraging the children to show each other their vulnerabilities? I want to show Toby, Sean, and Russell that it's safe to admit their fears, but perhaps I am just giving them ammunition.

"Let's pretend I told you I'm afraid of sharks," I tell them. "If you said, 'What? You're afraid of sharks?' I might feel bad, like I was dumb to be afraid. What might make me feel better?"

"I like sharks," Toby says.

I decide to take this as a constructive suggestion. "That might make me feel better," I say, "if it made me think that maybe sharks aren't so bad."

"If I say I'm scared of devils," Gwynn says, "and someone said, 'That's a really dumb idea,' I wouldn't like it. If they would just say, 'I'm scared of them, too. It's OK, 'cause they won't really hurt you,' that's better."

"I'm scared of mammoths," Nell says, adding another fear to her growing list. "They're kind of like elephants only they have curly things."

"They died in the Ice Age," Gwynn reassures her.

"Does that make you feel good or dumb?" I ask Nell.

"Good," she answers. "'Cause then I don't get to see them anymore."

"Last night I woke up," Timmy says, "and I was scared of a dinosaur." Timmy is often on a tangent to the subject of a discussion, but today, I notice, he is right on. "Mom says there are no dinosaurs," he adds.

"They're trying to make them again," Toby tells him.

"No," I say quickly. "Some scientists are talking about it, but they can't really do it."

"I don't feel like talking about dinosaurs," Timmy answers.

"Just keep it to yourself," Zoë advises him. "If you're scared, don't tell anyone. Then they won't tease you."

I hope Zoë is wrong and that I can convince these children it is safe to be vulnerable.

5

....

I Only Play with Five-Year-Olds

"Are you my best friend?" I hear Timmy ask Noah as the children come to the rug to hear a story.

"No," Noah answers. "I really only like to play with five-year-olds."

Startled, I stop straightening the books on the shelf and turn to look at the boys. Noah is one month older than Timmy and they often play together in the block area. But recently, I have seen that the older boys are starting to accept Noah. Yesterday, Sean, Noah's favorite, announced to me, "I'm playing with Noah!" remembering, no doubt, how upset I'd been when Noah was rejected.

But now, just as Noah is beginning to make a place for himself in their group, must he reject Timmy, the child one rung below him on the social ladder? Even at age four, does acceptance require finding someone else to keep out?

"Is that like saying, 'You can't play'?" I ask as the children settle at the rug. This rule is the cornerstone of our social order against which all behavior must be measured.

"W-w-well," Noah stammers, "Timmy can play with me, but I was just saying I like five-year-olds."

"When Timmy turns five," Nell says, "Noah might play with him."

"It's not fair," Russell says. "Because maybe by the time Timmy turns five, Noah won't be in this group."

In our multiage class, the fours may stay with me for a second year, while the fives move on to another teacher. Noah has given the children the impression that he is in the older group, but I am unwilling to let this misconception stand.

"Actually," I say, "Noah is four, too."

"But I'm older," Noah announces quickly.

"I think it's *not* fair that Noah likes five-year-olds," Toby says, "and I think it *is* fair because he doesn't want to play with Timmy." Toby is one of the oldest in the class, and he is just beginning to enjoy looking at a problem from different points of view.

"Sometimes I do want to play with him," Noah explains. "I like some four-year-olds a little bit, but just not as much as five-year-olds."

"Maybe Noah could choose between five-year-olds and four-year-olds," Zoë suggests. "Whichever one he played with more, that's what he has to keep playing with."

"I like to play with five-year-olds," Noah says without hesitation.

"Noah likes to play with five-year-olds," I say, unwilling to let this stand as the last word. "But is it fair for him to say he doesn't like to play with four-year-olds?"

"No," Zoë says, contradicting her own argument. "He can think to himself, 'I don't like to play with four-year-olds,' but he can't say it to them because he could hurt their feelings. And he could pretend that he likes four-year-olds more than he really does, but he could think inside, 'I don't like four-year-olds all that much.'"

I had thought that I was trying to encourage Noah to be generous to Timmy, as Sean has recently been generous to him. Instead, I seem to be encouraging him to learn to lie.

"Timmy," I ask, "did that hurt your feelings when Noah said he doesn't like four-year-olds all that much?"

"No," Timmy whispers, looking at the picture of a red dump truck on his blue sneakers.

"I don't like one idea of Zoë's," Russell says. "When she said, 'Whichever one she plays with more, she should keep playing with.' If he just likes five-year-olds, he won't like any four-year-olds and six-year-olds and seven-year-olds. My brother is eight and if I only liked five-year-olds, then I wouldn't like my brother! And I do like my brother."

"And what if the eight-year-olds wouldn't play with the five-year-olds?" I ask, driving this stake in a little deeper.

"I'd tell my mom!" Russell says.

"Tell a teacher!"

"You can tell the principal!"

"I agree with Zoë," Gwynn says. "You can pretend a person is your friend and think, inside, you don't like kids that age all that much."

"Noah," I say. "Now that you've had a chance to think about it, how do you feel?"

"I like four-year-olds that are older than me," Noah says, "and I like Russell more than Timmy, 'cause he's older than me. I like Timmy a little bit and I play with him a lot. And I like him. But I changed—I really do like four-year-olds."

I see the pressure I have put on him reflected in his attempts to change his feelings to meet our expectations. I tell myself that I'm just trying to understand his need to exclude, but in fact, I see that I am trying to make him change how he feels. Perhaps it is when I try to stop him before I understand him that I am teaching him to lie.

"I know!" Russell says. "Keep things that are mean to people to yourself! Because then they won't feel sad!"

"I agree!"

"Me, too!"

I begin to call for a vote on this new rule. Then I realize maybe we don't need a rule. Perhaps Toby has the right idea: it is fair and it isn't fair. As long as we're listening to each other, why do we have to choose?

6

....

Pretending to Die

Halloween is coming and a wide variety of monsters are creeping into the children's stories, needing to be defeated by their authors. Michelle, who had been telling stories about Madeline, the orphan girl, now has a new theme:

"Four Powerpuff Girls see a bad guy. They fire them. And then they go to the seashore. And they find a witch in a cave. They find a spaceship and they kill a witch and all the bad people."

Zoë chooses a fire-breathing dragon to be her opponent in the next chapter of "The Mystery of the Dead Unicorns," perhaps taking her weapon from Dorothy and the Wicked Witch:

"I'm the fairy princess and there's a fire-breathing dragon. We're supposed to fight it. I told the centaur to fight it because the centaur was really strong. Then I dump a big bucket of water on the dragon. The dragon runs away because it was so cold. It made the unicorns come back to life."

Scott is a five-year-old boy who prefers to play with the less competitive fours in the class. Today he has told his very first story and it follows the pattern the younger boys have been exploring: two Power Rangers go in a cave and find and kill a monster. When it's time to act it out, Sean plays the dying monster, falling slowly and dramatically to the floor. Several children cheer his performance, but Russell interrupts. "I don't like that," he says. "It reminds me of when my grandpa died and it makes me sad."

I am surprised that Russell, who recently announced he was not afraid of anything, allows himself to express sadness in such a public forum, and I wonder if his friends will support or ridicule him.

"Know what?" Zoë says. "I didn't like it when the dad died in *The Lion King*, 'cause it makes me scared about my dad."

"Me, too!"

"Me, too!"

There is a chorus of agreement from these children who have cheerfully been killing off monsters and bad guys on a daily basis since September.

"What I think we should do," Nell says, "is the people who don't like when they die, they could just, like, close their eyes."

"I think they should cover their ears," Gwynn adds, "so they don't hear people saying, 'the monster got dead.'"

"We could die," Toby suggests, "but we could just stand up, so he wouldn't think we were dying, like this." He stands stiffly, arms at his sides. "And we shouldn't say, 'Hooray! You died!'"

Just when I think I've figured out the code of rules for joining their group, I find I'm wrong. I wonder whether Toby, the monitor of "big boy" behavior, would have supported such an admission of vulnerability from Noah or Zoë.

"Maybe, like, when somebody died, they couldn't say, 'Ahhhh!' and they couldn't fall down when they shot them." Russell agrees with Toby.

"So, you don't mind if they're shot as long as they're not dead?" I ask.

"Uh huh," Russell agrees.

"If someone was in the street," Timmy says, "that's not a good idea—he might be hit by a car."

"That's true," I tell him, searching for a connection to our discussion. "You want to keep everyone safe so they're not really hurt."

"When they're dying," Zoë says, "they should go down slowly."

"Russell," I ask. "Does it matter how they look when they pretend to die or does it just matter whether we call it dying?"

"It matters what they look and what they call it dying," he answers.

"I have a great idea!" Zoë announces. "Russell, do you know, when someone dies, it's sad and beautiful at the same time? That means it can be beautiful when you die. I know it by dead unicorns are beautiful."

"Russell," I ask, "would that make you feel better about acting out stories with dying in them?"

"No," Russell says. "Because when my grandpa died there was a dump truck and they put him inside and they dumped him in a deep hole."

A shocked silence greets this description, but Zoë continues. "When I pretend to be dead, then we'll see if Russell thinks I look good or not."

I consider the possible outcomes of this scene: Russell could think Zoë does not look beautiful. Or he could think Zoë does look beautiful but he still wants to ban death scenes. Either way, Zoë is likely to be upset.

"No," I tell Zoë. "He doesn't want us to pretend to die because it reminds him of the time his grandfather really died and Russell was really sad."

"You mean he did die?" Zoë says, surprised.

"Is he still alive?" Timmy asks.

"No," Russell says.

"I'm really sad about my Sandy died," Timmy says. I know that he is referring to his infant baby sister. "Her body was made. She didn't breathe. She was just born."

"I'm sad about my cat died and it was not looking where it was going and then a car came and then it crashed and my daddy buried it," Michelle says.

"That's just what Timmy was worried about," I remind her.

"My grandpa died 'cause he had a heart attack," Noah says. "And Bubbles is still alive, my goldfish, but then I got a friend for

Bubbles and when he got black eyes, he died and now I got another fish and he's happy. He's still alive! I got Bubbles and another fish still swimming!"

"I have a new idea," Zoë says. "If they get killed, they get frozen into ice, is how they die!"

"So, we could say, 'frozen into ice' instead of calling it dying?" I ask, pleased that Zoë has come up with an idea that seems to encompass all the suggestions.

"Like when they get shot, they could stand up with their eyes closed!" Russell agrees with her plan.

"Let's try it," I say, returning to Scott's story. Sean reenters the circle with him. They act out the story again, but this time, when Scott raises his invisible gun and makes a soft "sh-sh-sh!" sound, Sean stands still with his arms at his sides until I say "the end," and the actors return to their seats.

The next story is Russell's.

"Russell wants to be a dragon," I announce, "and there is a lizard and a bad guy." Toby agrees to be the lizard, and Caleb, one of the fours, is the bad guy.

"The dragon has metal on him," I read from Russell's notebook. "Is that like armor?" I ask. He nods. "His friend is a lizard and he has an electric tongue. The lizard thundershocks the bad guy."

"How does he do that?" I ask. Children who take their stories from television can have a lexicon of action words and characters that I do not recognize, and I think it is important for them to be able to explain those words to those of us who have not seen the programs.

"He sticks his tongue out at him," Russell says.

I read the next sentence. "The dragon blows fire on him and he dies."

"Russell!" I say, surprised. "What do you want to do about that?"

Perhaps when Russell kills his own bad guy, he feels only relief, as when you vanquish an evil character in a dream. Only the death of someone else's monster can remind him of his grandfather.

"The dragon freezes the bad guy," Russell says.

Caleb, the burned and frozen bad guy, stands still with his arms at his sides and his eyes closed.

"The end," I announce.

7

....

Someone I Don't Love

"I can't give a present to someone I don't love!" Zoë explodes at Russell as we gather at the rug. "I love the girls and I don't really love the boys!"

"She's making pictures just for girls," Russell explains. "I don't like that, because it's no fair. I told her she should keep that to herself—it's mean."

"I think that's not fair," Brooke agrees. "'Cause that's like saying, 'You can't play.' "

"You know how you said on the playground, if you're playing with someone and you say, 'I won't play with you?' That's kind of like what Zoë said," Toby supports Russell. "She said, 'I won't give it to the boys.' "

"But that won't make *me* feel good," Zoë protests.

"I think she should make pictures for boys and girls," Ariel, one of the oldest girls in the class, suggests. "Which is more important? Not making feelings hurt is more important!"

"She should just give them to her family," Russell adds.

"She said she won't give it to the boys for no reason," Noah says. He's been playing with both the fours and the fives recently, but I've noticed that in discussions he tends to wait to hear what the three older boys say and then he makes a statement in support of them.

"I only made four pictures," Zoë argues.

"She could give two to girls and two to boys," Scott suggests. Scott likes to see the mathematical possibilities in a situation.

"She should make pictures for everybody who wanted one," Russell says.

I am surprised the boys even want Zoë's pictures. Recently, they have been rejecting any object or activity that has the slightest feminine aura, and I would imagine them throwing Zoë's unicorn pictures away if they had been offered.

"I don't like any of the boys!" Zoë announces. "I can't give a picture to somebody I don't love and I don't love any of the boys!"

"It's OK with me if you don't love everybody," I tell her. "But remember what Russell said, 'Keep things that are mean to people to yourself.' "

"Just send the pictures in the mail," Brooke suggests. "Then nobody knows."

"People who don't get them, I can make one for them," Russell offers.

"I think Russell could give them to the boys and I could give them to the girls," Zoë says.

I don't want to accept Zoë's premise that she can't give pictures to someone she doesn't love and that she doesn't like any boys. "What if I'm a boy and I like your unicorn pictures?" I ask.

"I'll make some for the whole class!" Toby offers enthusiastically. Toby loves to draw and would probably whip out a dozen unicorns in short order.

"Me, too!"

"Me, too!"

"I want to make some. Even at our houses!" Nell says. "And we should make lots of them, even for people we don't know very good!"

"Even if they're from far, far away!" Michelle adds.

"We could make pictures for the whole school!" Even Scott, who rarely draws, is excited about the project.

"Know what I'm going to do?" Zoë says. "Give them to the girls when the boys aren't looking."

"Maybe when they all go in the girls' bathroom they can give them to each other and roll them up and put them in their pockets!" Russell suggests.

I preferred the previous mood of generosity to the new plan of secrecy. I imagine all my girls trying to get permission to go to the bathroom during recess and I start to envision problems. "You can't do that during school," I say, "but you could mail them when you're at home."

"I don't have their addresses," Zoë says.

"Mom and Dad have the class list," I argue.

"No," she answers.

Now I'm in a corner and I need to find a way out. Once again, I find myself trying to control the outcome of the discussion, insisting that Zoë change her original idea. I could have ended with the generosity of the enthusiastic picture-making project. Or I could have accepted the idea that the girls could give each other pictures privately, even if not all at once in the bathroom. In either case, Zoë has received a clear message that her pictures are highly valued by both girls and boys and that it is important for her to consider the feelings of the children who feel left out of her gift giving.

"It seems as though most people feel, Zoë, as though it's OK to give a picture to a friend, but you have to be careful not to hurt someone's feelings when you do it," I say.

"Like right in front of them," Brooke agrees with my summation, "if a boy's right next to them."

"If she quietly made a picture for a friend, that would be OK," Scott agrees.

I decide to leave it there. Before Zoë can believe that "not making feelings hurt is most important," she needs to see how things look from another person's point of view. I must trust that eventually our discussions will lead her there.

8

....

Shouting

"Don't shout at me!"

Zoë is shouting herself, and I look up from the round table where Michelle is dictating a story to me. Gwynn and Ariel sit across from Zoë, with tiny beads scattered all over the table in front of them. They look as though they are dressed for three separate environments: Gwynn, in her white dress with tiny flowers, always looks clean, even after she has been painting all morning. Ariel wears a sweat suit and her hands are covered with colored marker where they have smudged her pictures. Zoë wears the same vest every day, purple with a small pink unicorn.

"What's the matter, Zoë?" I ask.

"They screamed at me not to bump the table!" Zoe is crying now and is hard to understand.

"I can hear you better when you don't shout," I tell them all.

"She made us mess up our bead patterns!" Ariel explains. "We just told her not to bump the table and then she did it some more."

"But they were screaming at me!" Zoë defends herself.

"What would you like to have happen now?" I ask Zoë.

"I want to go home! I want a new school!"

"I can't do that for you," I say. "I can only try to make our school as good for you as possible. Is there anything you want to have happen here?"

Zoë takes a deep breath, as though reminding herself to calm down. "I want them not to shout at me if I bump the table by accident," she says, speaking more quietly now. "They can say, 'Please don't do that.' Then I won't get mad at them."

I'm glad I asked. Zoë's willingness to join this group of girls is new and her relationship with them is fragile. If I had tried to smooth over the problem by imposing my own solution, she might have withdrawn or remained defensive.

The girls agree, relieved to have a solution to the problem, and start to pick up the spilled beads.

9

....

Roaring, Again

"Sean was roaring at me!" Zoë shouts as the children tumble in from recess, pulling off their snow boots and demanding help with shoelaces.

"What did you do about it?" I ask, hoping she didn't slug him. I've been talking with Zoë's parents daily about her self-control, and I'd like to be able to give them a good report.

"I told him I hope he has a bad dream," she tells me.

"Good job," I say, as I give her a hug. "I'm glad you didn't hit him. We'll talk about it when everyone comes to the rug."

"Sean," I say as he sits down to put on his shoes. "Zoë says you were making scary noises at her when she told you not to."

"I was doing it to myself," Sean says, appearing to talk to some dust on the floor in front of him.

"I don't think so," I answer. I know immediately that I will never win this battle, trying to tell Sean what he was thinking. Again, I'm ready to jump in to protect Zoë before I've even heard the whole story.

"Sean," I continue. "I've told you before that it's not OK to scare someone who tells you what he or she is afraid of."

"Zoë keeps bothering us," Russell defends his friend.

"We're roaring, and she keeps following us," Toby agrees.

"I needed to tell them I didn't like them roaring," Zoë explains.

Now I am confused. Was Zoë following them, the old girls' game of provoking and then telling on the boys? My assumption that she was the innocent victim is shaken.

"And she keeped on following us and she keeped on telling us," Toby adds.

"I want to play on the hill where they are," Zoë says.

Russell speaks quietly, his head down. "We said, 'Come look at something special,' and then we roared at her."

Once again I shift my view of innocence and guilt. "Russell," I say. "Thank you for telling the truth when it was really hard."

"Once I had a friend and we liked to roar," Michelle says.

"That's fine," I tell her. "What's not OK is roaring at someone who doesn't like it."

"Zoë could change her mind," Russell says.

I picture the boys roaring at her each day just to check. "If she does," I say, "she'll let us know. Until then, don't do it." I look at my three culprits. "You know, I've been working with Zoë on not hitting. I told her that if she hits, she has to play next to me for fifteen minutes so I can be sure she settles down. Well, if you tease her, you should play near me, too. That's only fair."

They don't argue. Still, I sense the futility of my focus on trying to determine who is the perpetrator and who is the victim through this constantly changing story. In the Calvin and Hobbes cartoons, Calvin, reprimanded by his teacher, retreats into his fantasy, where as Spaceman Spiff he captures the aliens who are trying to find the secret formula for an atomic napalm neutralizer. Similarly, I suspect that my seemingly fair consequences just convince Zoë and Toby that I do not really understand them.

10
....

An Expert on Teasing

I decide to call an expert. My brother is now a social worker, mediating child custody cases for the Oregon divorce court. On the next weekend, I dial his number.

"Peter," I say, when I hear his voice. "I have a girl in my class who hates to be roared at. So, of course there are several boys who love to roar at her, just to see her scream and run to the teacher. I've tried to make them stop, but that doesn't work: it doesn't help the teaser with his need to hurt or help the girl to stop being a scapegoat. I want to find a better way to deal with it. So tell me," I pause, searching for the right words. "Why did you used to tease me so much?"

He begins slowly. "It's a hostility thing, a way of inflicting pain. Since there's no blood on the carpet, the consequences aren't severe. You're not doing physical harm, so you can say to yourself, 'This is harmless.'" He pauses.

"Keep talking," I encourage him. "This is helpful."

"There are certain people you can't tease," he says. "There's no point teasing people who don't get furious or hurt, though it can be fun to tease people who tease back."

"Why did you tease me so much?" I ask again.

"The psychologist Ivan Boszormenyi-Nagy says that when some injustice is done to us, there's a debt we're owed. We attempt to collect on our debt from somebody else. He calls it 'destructive entitlement.' I was twice displaced," he continues, picking up speed. "First, I had Mom all to myself. Then Dad came home from the war. Then you were born.

"Teasing Dad was not a winner of an idea. But you were a dream come true as a teasee. Remember the time I told you that if you kept beating the orange juice long enough, it would turn into a Popsicle?" His voice brightens over the telephone wire. "You were so mad when you tried it and found out it wasn't true," he adds cheerfully.

I remember: that hot, flushed feeling, knowing I'd been tricked again. Like being tickled, when for the first moment it may seem like it's going to be fun, that the attention will be worth the discomfort, but when it gets out of your control, the laughter becomes tears. Still, since you're laughing, there's no one else to blame.

I think about Toby and Sean, both younger brothers, and wonder what debts they are owed and whether I can help them collect on these debts in a more constructive way.

Eyeball-Head

Coming in from recess, I see Timmy alone, holding back tears. "Toby called me 'eyeball-head,' " Timmy tells me quietly, when I ask what is wrong.

"That reminds me of my brother," I say. He looks up at me, surprised. "I'll tell you that story at meeting."

I am aware of a subtle change in my attitude this morning. My curiosity has been awakened and I want to know if my boys feel they are owed something, too. I'm not out to prove anyone's theory, but I am aware that wanting to understand makes me feel better than wanting to blame.

"This is a story about when I was a little girl," I tell the children, when they're all at the rug. Timmy, who has been lying on the floor, rocks himself up to a sitting position, Nell puts down the book she's just pulled off the shelf, and the other children stop wiggling and look at me expectantly. This is their favorite kind of story.

"When I was little," I tell them, "I had a big brother. Well, I still do—now he's grown up. He's fifty-eight."

"How old are you?" Nell asks.

"I'm fifty-three," I say, feeling old. Her parents are about half my age. But I'm feeling brave today, and a bit bold, so I go on.

"When I was your age, my brother loved to tease me. He liked to call me names. One day, he called me a hypotenuse and it made me so mad! I didn't know what it was, but I was sure it must be really bad."

"What is it?" Toby asks.

"It's part of a triangle," I say. Quickly, I draw a diagram of right angles and diagonal lines. There's a geometry lesson they'll remember, I think as I draw. Won't their fifth-grade teacher be surprised when they already know what a hypotenuse is.

"Toby called me 'eyeball-head,' " Timmy says.

"Me and Sean was teasing Timmy," Toby admits.

"I'm really proud of you, Toby," I tell him. "It can be hard to admit when you've done something wrong."

"Timmy can say, 'Stop!' and if he doesn't stop he can tell the teacher." Brooke applies our standard rule to the problem.

"Timmy did say stop," Russell says. "But Toby kept on going. If Timmy made a mad face, Toby might stop and it would be all over."

"Just go somewhere else," Scott suggests. I realize that I've never seen Scott in an argument.

"If you make a funny face," Nell says, "he might forget about it." Maybe Nell gets along so easily because she can good-naturedly laugh off whatever she doesn't like.

"I asked my brother why he used to tease me so much," I tell the children. "He told me two things. First, he said that he was angry because he was the oldest and he had my mother all to himself. Then I was born and he was mad that he had to share her attention." I decide quickly to leave out the part about my father's return. I'm afraid that once I speak the words *return from the war,* the subject of entitlement will be gone and we'll be comparing grandfathers' war stories for the rest of the morning.

I continue my story. "My brother told me that I was easy to tease—I cried whenever he teased me, so he could be mean to me without getting in too much trouble."

Toby interrupts. "My brother and sister told me, 'We're gonna get a Popsicle and you aren't.' "

"Did you punch them in the face?" Sean asks.

"I kicked them," Toby answers. "Then they told on me and I got in trouble."

The room is silent as we take in his story of the unjustly accused.

"That happened to me, too," I tell Toby. "My brother would tease me, I would hit him, and my mother would send me to my room. It felt so unfair!"

Zoë speaks for the first time. "I don't understand why he's, like, teasing you and then you hit him back and then you're the one to get in trouble. I don't understand why he would tease you. But I know how he felt, because I only got to be with my mother by myself for two years and then they had my baby brother. And then he got most of the attention and I didn't get any of it!"

"Did you ever feel like teasing him?" I ask.

"Well, sometimes I felt like hitting him and pushing him and throwing him in the garbage, but I didn't do it," she answers.

"Well, maybe that's how my brother felt the day he told me if I beat orange juice long enough, it would turn into a Popsicle," I say. "I beat it and beat it and beat it, but it didn't work. Then he laughed at me."

They look at me, puzzled. "You have to put it in the freezer." I explain.

They smile. Now they remember.

"I guess it's better than hitting me or pushing me or putting me in the garbage," I say.

Zoë laughs. "Then you would have to turn into something different! Like when something's broken, you put it in the trash truck, so they can make it into things again. And you would be one of those things!"

I imagine being recycled and compacted, like a plastic milk jug, into a fleece jacket or a park bench.

"I like it when I'm in the pool and someone says, 'Na, na, na, boo, boo!' " Sean says. "'Cause you know what? I can dive under water!"

"I like it when my cat teases me," Gwynn says.

"Sometimes teasing is a way of saying, 'Play with me,' " I explain. "But in school, as Brooke says, when you say 'stop,' the teaser must stop. If the person being teased likes it, then it's a game and you can play it."

I know there is more to Zoë and Toby than just destructive entitlement. But if trying to understand the point of view of the teaser helps me to be curious rather than simply critical, perhaps it can have the same effect on them.

12
....

I Can't Be Friends
with a Total Stranger

The morning five-year-old Cassie comes to visit, Zoë has a bad day. Making snow angels outdoors, Zoë's socks get wet. After recess, she starts to put on her gym shoes. "My socks are wet! I hate wet socks!" she screams. She pauses a moment and then adds dramatically, "This is the worst day of my whole life!"

Timmy laughs nervously. Zoë flings her gym shoe, hitting him squarely on the head.

"You stop that!" I tell her quickly, adding my stern teacher's voice to the shouting and the tense chatter.

"You expect everyone to be perfect!" Zoë yells back at me.

"No," I say, wondering briefly if she is right. I do ask myself if I demand too much, insisting that no one be excluded. But I quickly decide this question is irrelevant to the present subject. "You can tell Timmy not to laugh at you, but you must not throw things at him!" I tell her.

At lunchtime, when Cassie's visit is over, I go straight to the office. "I can't possibly take a new child!" I tell the principal. "I can barely handle the ones I have now!"

At the end of the day, while Zoë is putting on her jacket, she says, "Cassie can't come here! If she came here, everyone would play with her! And then what?"

Why didn't I think of that? Of course Zoë would worry about the effect a new girl would have on Zoë's own fragile place in the group. For a moment, I ponder the frequency with which I identify and empathize with only the new child and not with the one who fears displacement. In fact, I am doing exactly what Zoë fears—looking at things from only the eyes of the newest child.

"You're still a new kid to everyone," Gwynn tells Zoë, before I am able to figure out what to say.

"Do you think your friends won't like you any more?" I ask Zoë, aware of the slight shift in my attitude as I begin to wonder what it is like to be the one who is trying to keep another out.

"Because Cassie would be the last to come, she'd be new to them," Zoë explains.

"No," Gwynn says. "I would keep being your friend, Zoë, but I would play with both of you."

I wonder, briefly, if I need to say more about Timmy and the shoe. But Timmy seems settled and interested in our conversation, and right now I don't want to take away from the important lesson Zoë has just received from Gwynn.

The next morning, I tell the children that Cassie will be in the class down the hall. "I felt bad," Zoë says, "because you know I can't be friends with a total stranger! 'Cause how can I communicate with her! I can't be friends with a stranger until I know a lot about them—she doesn't talk at all."

"That's just because Cassie was scared," Gwynn explains.

"She was shy," Brooke adds. "Just like Nell and Michelle and me. I was shy."

"No!" Ariel says, disbelieving.

"Yes! I was!" Brooke insists.

"I'm friends with everyone in the whole school," Nell says. "Even the people who I don't know."

Little Nell does not have to talk to make a new friend. She just smiles and starts playing. Zoë, with her extraordinary vocabulary, does not have Nell's knack of assuming she's friends with children she doesn't know yet.

"So, Zoë," I say, "you thought that no one would play with you if Cassie came because she would be the newest?"

"Yeah," Zoë agrees. "All the girls would play with her."

"When Zoë first came," Gwynn admits, "I sort of felt like Ariel wasn't gonna play with me."

"Of course I would, Gwynn! You're my bestest friend!" Ariel pauses. "Well, maybe that would make someone else feel sad. So all my friends are my bestest friends," she adds, tactfully.

"So, you wouldn't stop playing with Gwynn?" I ask.

"No!" Ariel exclaims. "'Cause she was in my preschool! 'Cause we've been together a long time!"

"Ariel did sometimes play with Zoë," Gwynn says. "And sometimes I wouldn't even see her. But sometimes, when Ariel's gone and Zoë's here, I can play with Zoë. And when Zoë's not here, I can play with Ariel."

"Or if we're both here, Gwynn could play with both of us!" Ariel adds happily.

"In my old preschool," Russell says, "I had tons of friends that were boys. And someone who wasn't my friend was takin' away all my friends. And then I had no friends except one. And it was Sean!" He puts his arm around Sean, who is sitting next to him on the rug.

"I didn't know you were friends in preschool," I tell Sean and Russell. They smile at each other, remembering the old days, when they were young.

When Toby told Noah "We don't like you," he was trying to make a place for himself in the preexisting friendship between Sean and Russell. When Noah told Timmy "I really only like to play with five-year-olds," he was working hard to enter the older boys' group. Now Zoë "can't play with a total stranger" just when she is trying to establish a friendship with Ariel and Gwynn. When they are most vulnerable and least confident of the positions they strive for, each of these children is most determined to keep a newer child out. Must exclusion, I wonder, be the price of a secure place in the group?

13
....

In the Wilderness

During Christmas break, I describe my puzzlement about exclusion to my friend Kate, who works in a program for troubled teens. As we drink our coffee and look out her window at the New England mountains, I tell her about my big boys, Toby, Russell, and Sean, the little ones, Noah and Timmy, and my wild card, Zoë.

"If you want to learn about exclusion," she says, "you should talk with my kids!"

"Would they talk to me?" I ask.

"They love to talk about issues like that," she tells me. "I'll ask them if they're interested in being a part of your research."

So, two weeks later, I return to the mountains. Now, snow covers the ground, and Kate and her group of ten high school students arrive at the empty dining hall bundled in winter jackets, scarves, and snow boots.

I set a box of enormous chocolate cookies and a stack of napkins in the middle of the table and set up my tape recorder in front of me. I know that Kate has explained to them that I'm doing research on exclusion, but I don't want them to mistake me for a therapist.

I tell them about the day Zoë threw her shoe at Timmy because she was afraid that Cassie would take her place with the other girls in the group. "Has an adult ever done anything that helped with a problem of exclusion?" I ask Kate's group of teens.

"I had two things, actually," Kirk says, folding his napkin into tiny squares. "I took karate for about ten years. My sensei really kind of built my self-esteem. You know, he was stern with me but he became one of my close friends; he was fatherly to me. I think it really built who I became or it gave me something to build on. 'Cause when I was younger, I didn't have that.

"Advice didn't help," he continues. "The more people gave me advice, the more I said, 'God, I just wish I could do that,' or 'I wish that was the way it was.' But it wasn't. You know what I mean? And it's not like I wouldn't want people to say that to me; it just didn't do anything.

"And then another thing an adult did for me which was more negative was my guitar teacher. He was thirty. He got me into smoking pot. And that became my way of getting out of exclusion because everybody drew me in because I was a little kid who smoked pot. And that's how in the beginning I started to get into drugs and I got in trouble. I went to a wilderness program."

I have heard about the therapeutic programs that take students into the wilderness, teaching them survival skills while they also teach them to be constructive members of the group. "Will you tell me about wilderness?" I ask. "Did it help you?"

"A good amount of us came in the same way," Kirk answers. "You don't have any images about what to wear, because everybody was basically wearing the same exact thing. It's like when people start to clique together, it's broken up because you're in a small group so you need everybody's support. So two people can't be best friends and exclude everyone else, 'cause then people will get hurt, because it was wilderness. So the main thing that was different was I'm not saying you would die but you can not do what you needed to do without every single person doing their share. Like when some people came in, at first they didn't see that. You know, I didn't see that at first. I thought, I can do my thing, you know, just do a lot and you know, the other guy didn't have to do as much, because I would do what he didn't do. And then I began to realize that everybody needed to do something, because it wouldn't have worked. So everybody was really close because we were all doing the same exact thing. We were all working together. There wasn't a leader, because everybody was leading in some way. So it was just a different experience. If you had somebody that was lower, then it would hold the whole group back. So everybody would go down to that level to help that person.

"We formed a language. We had a kinship with each other that I've never had with anyone." Kirk begins to tear his napkin into squares along the folded lines. "One kid saved my life. I fell down an icy hill and it's this thing that we developed with each other that was unbreakable. Now I'll probably never talk to them again in my life but I still feel a connection with them, you know what I mean? It's weird."

Everybody would go down to that level to help that person. That is my image of the kind of class I want to have: the children helping Zoë to trust our group, and she, in turn, giving us her stories, her imagination, her creative solutions to problems; the group teaching Toby that he can gain more by being a contributing member than he can by trying to get the most of everything.

Andrew, a heavyset blond, slouching in his chair, speaks after a short pause, "For me, it was in middle school, it got to the point where people were, like, actually getting into fistfights and, like, beating the crap out of each other just to move up in this whole little group thing, and it just got to the point where it was ridiculous." Andrew looks at his large hands in front of him on the table while he thinks. "And, like, I got thrown out of school. I didn't go to school for most of seventh and eighth grade, and I was put in a program out in the wilderness for a year, like Kirk did, and there, there were no groups, you were your own group with the five or six people that they stuck you with, and you learned to depend on everybody else. To live, I mean if you couldn't depend on somebody, then the chances of you living were like slim to none. So we eventually learned to get along with each other. It took a while and it was really tough, but there I kind of figured out that if you are excluding people, you're really kind of like excluding yourself from being in a group." He looks at me, bear-like, with his head down. "I don't know if that makes sense, you know."

I wonder if he means that only a group that includes everyone can give him the security that comes with knowing he is accepted for who he really is.

"Can you tell me how you learned that in wilderness?" I ask.

Andrew looks at his hands and then briefly his soft brown eyes look directly at me. "At first, I was by myself," he says. "I didn't work, so I didn't get any food. I thought nobody cared about me. Then a scorpion stung me and I had to go to the group to get help. That's when I started to figure it all out."

Kirk breaks the remains of his cookie into tiny pieces. "I think that with exclusion, it doesn't really matter what people do for you," he says. "It just matters about you. And people can do things to help you get to that point. Like my guitar teacher inadvertently changed my life, you know what I mean? And the people in my wilderness program definitely, they were really big people in my life and I think they did a lot for me, 'cause they believed in me, too, when I didn't believe in myself. They're not necessarily holding your hand or telling you that it's gonna be all right, but they are there to walk with you, you know what I mean?"

14

· · · · · · · · · · ·

Under Her Wing

"Actually," Kallie says, "I've been in the position of being excluded and it's been really tough."

I bend close to hear her. Her face is red and blotchy, and I worry that she is about to break into hives. "I feel scared," she says. "It's something that's real hard. Looking at other people, you want to be like other people, you start dressing like them. I don't know. I think people are real threatened by other people when they have no chance at being friends with their friends."

"Has an adult ever helped?" I ask.

"I never really talked about it," she says, looking at the floor in front of her. "I tried to avoid it. I'd think about it to myself, in my room, sometimes. My parents didn't want to hurt me. I'd just keep on going, seem friendly." She rubs her face. I want to reach out and stop her but I know I must restrain myself.

"I actually did talk to adults," Brian says, "and no one ever, ever helped. It was just that after a long time, I was getting physically beaten up almost every day. In the hospital once. And it was just one of those things where the kids really don't care when the adults told them to stop. When they got in trouble for it, they'd just be more careful. Outside forces didn't do anything."

I look at Brian, trying to see if I can find some obvious reason for his getting bullied. He has dark hair, pale skin, blue eyes, and long lashes, with a slender gentleness that may be appealing to girls but that could strike boys as lacking in toughness. He speaks confidently, without Kallie's apparent anxiety.

"I actually had to figure it out for myself," he says. "Some people had told me some of the things that I did eventually figure out. But until I figured it out for myself, it didn't work."

"If you were going to give advice to Kallie," I say, "what would you tell her?"

"The way I got out of it probably wasn't the most helpful," he answers. "I kept my mouth shut at almost all times and I almost got to the point where I wasn't noticed at all. I still do that."

"For me," Travis says, "I think it's all about what's inside of you. You're your attitude. You can be like fine, since people think I'm an outcast, I'm an outcast; you let it happen, roll over on your back. But for me, I was a fat kid, and, like, I just didn't let it bother me. I was always one of the most popular kids. You just, like, laugh it off, you just ignore them: all right, that's their opinion."

"I agree with Travis," Nalasa, a girl with mocha skin and an ethnicity that I can't quite place, says. "Like, if you feel that you're a person who's popular, or you feel you're a person who's not popular, that's how it's going to be. Like, in elementary and in high school, young kids are very easily influenced, and in elementary school, I feel like I, too, was very easily influenced by parents, your neighborhood, and so forth. But once I broke out of that group and asserted myself, what he said was true, when people say things to me, I don't take it personally, I don't really care. I think that's a lot of how I go through my day, like a lot of people, their opinions don't matter to me. That's not a good thing, but I don't really care unless it's someone who I know has a clear perspective on the situation or who's a close friend to me or a teacher. Otherwise, their comments, it's in one ear and out the other or something like that."

"Like, that's what my mom told me," Kirk says, twirling his pen around his finger and catching it deftly. "You have to kind of let it roll off your back, and I really tried, but when I look back on it, I was so obsessed with who was higher, I was just, like, shooting myself in the foot. When I look back on it, kindergarten through eighth grade was all about image: how you dressed, how you looked and what you did. It wasn't about who you are."

"I had a nickname," Kallie says, "that was named after a sumo wrestler on TV." I look at her, startled. She is not a skinny teen, like some of the girls around the table, but she is not heavy. She turns her head away from me, perhaps hiding tears, so again I lean closer to catch her words.

"What they don't realize," she continues, "is that when they gain so much power to destroy somebody else and to demoralize somebody else, they don't treat them as a human being. I still, to this day, can't let go of these things. I never talk about them. I just haven't got to the point where I can even talk to somebody about it—how much it hurt me and how much it still hurts me."

Kallie's isolation stands out among these teens who feel so comfortable telling me about their problems.

"In elementary school," Laura, a large girl in an oversized shirt, says, "what really helped me—it was just accepting who I was. My mother was consoling me and letting me know that I'm not alone. There's a lot of kids out there that get hurt; it's not just me. The bad thing about being made fun of is that the attention is on you 100 percent. But it makes me more comfortable to feel like I wasn't the only one. I'm not alone. People don't just hate me. And my mother told me she was ridiculed as a child and now I hear that everybody was made fun of at one time or another and that makes me feel like I'm not the only one; like there's nothing wrong with me."

"I made friends with other kids who were already made fun of," Dylan says. He looks Asian, maybe Korean, but is tall, and he sits next to a pretty Asian girl, his arm over the couch behind her. "And those kids already were part of a group and I'd make friends with them, too, and then maybe there would be another kid they'd make fun of and my turn was over. That was how I saw it."

"Have you ever been the one on the inside, keeping others out?" I ask. "I'd like to know more about what that's like."

"This summer," Jaimie says, "when I was here for the first time, I was kind of entangled in, like, a group of friends." She puts her blonde hair behind her ear. "It was four of us and we had a name for us and it was, like, all our own names put together.

And we didn't keep to ourselves but when it came to, like, one-on-one time, no one else was invited. And we kind of all had these necklaces. And I ended up, there was another girl we didn't want in our group, and I ended up cutting the necklace off her. Like, that's an example of a really cruel thing that I'd done. But it was a real wake-up call and it was, like, I saw something that I hadn't seen before. Like, the impact I had on people. And not only the person that I did cut the necklace from but also those girls that were around me." She bats her large circular earring.

"What happened?" I ask her. I wonder how that wake-up call came about.

"I ended up getting in trouble for it, which I really resented at first, but I think it really did free me to look at it."

"What was it about getting in trouble that forced you to see that?" I ask again. I have the feeling that Jaimie is telling me her carefully worked out ideas, but I can't find the questions to help her explain to me what she went through.

"I guess for a long time I didn't feel like I was in control of things and the only thing that I could control were my relationships, even though I couldn't control, like, myself. I didn't feel like there was anything worth living for or waking up in the morning. But I needed, like, a sense of control in my life. And that's where the people around me came in. Just like the littlest thing, those were the things that filled that void of control."

"So, how do you get into that position of power?" I ask.

"I think I make people want to fear me," Jaimie says. "I don't think I'm intimidating in a physical or in a fighting sense. But my friends say I am intimidating, like making vulnerable people want to give in. They tell me they worry about what I'll say about them behind their backs."

"I was pretty much always in the inside," Ashley, the Asian girl sitting on the couch next to Dylan, says. "But there was a time in fourth grade when I switched schools and everyone had already established friends, so it was a little hard. But the most popular girl, I guess she kind of took me under her wing, as her project, so it wasn't like a struggle for me, 'cause she liked me."

"How do you get to decide who's in and who's out?" I ask.

"This sounds really bad," Ashley says. "You have to have the ability to, like, hurt people, because people don't ever want to be hurt. I don't know too many people who want to be hurt, unless they're masochistic or whatever."

"But then wouldn't they leave you alone?" I ask.

"Well, I think there's also something intriguing about a group," Ashley goes on. "Like, here's a perfect example which is going on right now. There's a girl named Nadia and she does not have any social skills whatsoever. And she asked to go to the prom in my limo with my friends and she said, 'Whatever you do for prom can I come?'" Ashley leans back on the couch and glances briefly at Dylan, who rolls his eyes.

"And I was like, 'I don't see why not. I don't see a problem with that.' And when I talked with my friends, they have been for the past month thinking of elaborate ways in which they can tell her no, she can't come, there's just no way. And then they're like, 'If she's gonna come, then I'm gonna get a different limo.'

"And I was like, 'You guys, she doesn't have any friends. Like who else is she gonna go in a limo with?' And, like, I don't know, I don't think I'm mean at heart all the time. And I understand and I feel bad for her. But at the same time, what my friends are saying about how she gets on their nerves, she does that to me, too. And I usually end up biting my tongue, 'cause I feel bad for her. 'Cause I can't imagine what it would be like to not have friends. And I don't know, 'cause if I didn't have friends, I don't know what I'd do. So, today, when one of my friends said to her, 'Who told you that you can come in our limo?' and she said, 'Ashley,' and then my friend went to me and was, like, so mad at me and said, 'You better find a way to tell her that she's not going in our limo.'

"But I was like, 'She doesn't have any friends. So what do you want me to do about it?' And I walked away, so it was like, I don't know, I feel really bad, and I hate that."

"Are you worried about sticking up for her?" I ask. "Will it hurt your reputation?"

"No, I don't think so, because I have a pretty good ability to make people feel bad. Later on, I was like, 'I don't care. I'll go in a limo by myself then. I won't even go in the same limo as you. And you're my date!'

"And he was like, 'No, no, no. It's fine, it's fine.'" She glances again at Dylan, giving him a half smile.

"That sounds like you're taking her under your wing," I say. My time with them is almost over, and the group starts to break up. But Brian and Ashley both hang around as I put away my notebook and gather my jacket and hat, preparing for the sharp bite of mountain winter.

"Today some guys in my dorm did pretty much everything they could to force me to fight," Brian tells me. "Which didn't happen. But I was definitely in an awkward position and I ended up having to leave and come over here."

"You used to fight, though, right?" I ask, remembering his brief phrase about being in the hospital.

"I used to have no choice and usually I didn't fight back very much. But I definitely got beat up. There was no point in fighting back—it was hopeless."

"Why do the kids in your dorm want you to fight?" I ask.

"I guess they feel that that's their way of exerting power and they don't like that everybody else is running their life, so they make their own little hallway. That's their way of thinking."

"What are you doing that bothers them?" I ask him.

"Being there," he answers. "I'm not part of their group; therefore they don't want me there. I don't listen to them. That bothers them. I'm in the tech crew group at the theater. Maybe it's my personal prejudice, but I don't think the tech crew puts as much of a group face on putting people down as the other groups. But at the same time, it's kind of like whichever group you pick, it's going to affect the way you handle yourself. Choosing which group you want to be a part of is who you are. So, you have to make sure you seek out your own group."

"What are you going to do about it?" I ask him.

"That's a real good question," he answers slowly, looking down at his unlaced hiking boots. "I've been thinking about that all day. I wish I had a better answer. I was thinking about talking to our adviser to see what I can do. I don't know, at this point. I don't want to get them more annoyed. I don't want to feel threatened in my own room. It's a hard position."

He picks up his jacket and walks away.

"What do you think he should do?" I ask Ashley. "What can a person do who's being bullied like that?"

"I think, like, they need to just find one good person in the crowd of people that has the upper hand and let them know what's going on. And sort of like have them take them under their wing. And I've seen people do it and it works. Like this kid Rob—he's popular, he's nice, he's funny, he's smart, and everyone, I don't care who it is, loves him. And he's always kind of been rooting for the underdog. And, like, I think people are sort of intimidated, but he's such a great person and it's just like, I don't know, I think people need to be taken under other people's wings. There are always some good people."

I wonder who, in my class, has a wing large enough to encompass Zoë.

15

All on My Terms

In Zoë's stories, she is a fairy princess and her friends protect her from danger as she searches for the murderer of the dead unicorns:

"The fairy princess flew over to Eunice the Unicorn's house and knocked at the door. And out came a white unicorn with two gold babies at her feet. The fairy princess said, 'Hello, Eunice. Are all my friends inside?'

" 'Yes, they are,' said Eunice. And as the door opened, she saw all her friends."

In real life, however, Zoë is both excluded and excludes others. Her fear that her friends could turn against her leads her to make accusations that alienate them and that isolate her. So, when Kate tells me that Ashley had enjoyed talking with me, I grab the opportunity to hear from someone who seems so confident that she has the group under her control. "Do you think she would talk with me again?" I ask Kate.

"I think so," Kate says. "You might want to ask her about her punk group back home."

A couple of weeks later, I sit in the school lounge with Kate, Ashley, and Dylan. Ashley has new, bright red streaks covering some of her black hair. Dylan is tall and strong and doesn't fit the stereotype of the slender Asian intellectual. He seems relaxed and comfortable with her.

"I come from a really exclusive group," Ashley says. "Like my scene back home is a punk scene and I cannot think of too many groups that are more exclusive than that. But I know so many different kinds of people. I don't know. When I came here to school, I feel more excluded than I've ever felt before. I don't know why that is. Well, I guess like here you're told to look at so many things about yourself, and there's just so many things to look at, and I guess I feel more excluded probably because I exclude myself. It's just like nothing's on my terms, I guess. I think I get to know less people because I feel so forced. This is my third high school and my natural instinct when I switch schools is to get to know everyone. And I usually get to know at least 500 kids before half a year is up. The philosophy of this school is, like, to open yourself up, show humility, and live by your conscience, and in doing that you're supposed to be more open to people. I guess it just doesn't work for me."

She pauses; I decide to wait and see what she says next.

"I guess I go to my friends at home for security," she says. "I don't know, I guess I know that no matter what, I can always go back to them. They're always gonna be there. And I just call to tell them what day I'm coming home and they're just waiting for me. There's about thirty of them, and they all just wait in the same place. If I'm not sure if they're gonna be there that day 'cause it's cold or raining out, I just call the pay phone and they'll pick up."

"What does it mean to be punk, besides the colored hair and the music?" I ask Ashley.

"I can't define that," she says. "I guess punk attitude is non-conformity and just like at the same time, a certain amount of acceptance and a respect for difference. Although, and I wrote my junior thesis on this, there is a huge contradiction because although that's what we try to be, it usually ends up backfiring.... I'm the only girl in my group and any time a girl tries to enter and, like, interact with many of my guy friends, I get so defensive, and I, like, flip out! And I can't stand it, and I'll be sitting with my friend Jon and say, like, 'So, what do you think of her? She's annoying, right?'

" 'Yup, she's annoying. I can't stand her,' he'll say. And then we'll just exclude her."

She pauses. "It's horrible, now that I think about it." She sounds surprised and truly dismayed at herself.

"Why do you do that?" I ask her. "What are you afraid of?"

"I want all the attention to be on me!" She answers without hesitating. "There's a level of respect that I get for being the only girl. And I don't want that taken away, ever, and it's funny, because I walk around the city and I've been in three schools and I've been to a couple of elementary schools and I've played soccer on a bunch of teams, and I know a lot of people in the city. And I'll be walking around and people come up to me and they'll know who I am, but I won't know them. And I definitely feel I'm on top of the world when people come up and they're like, 'Are you Ash?' 'cause I have my little punk rock name tattooed on my shoulder. And people know who I am and it's just like this stupid sense of entitlement that I feel any time someone challenges that, I don't know. I get threatened, and I feel like I have to retaliate in some way. And it's funny, 'cause I can usually manipulate it so I get people on my side. Like, this girl was like, 'Who are you? I don't think we've met?' and I was just like, 'That's right, you don't know *me*?' and just like . . ."

Dylan, who has been sitting quietly on the couch next to Ashley with his arm casually around her shoulder, sits up. "Oh, man! Those guys should just say, 'Who wants to know *you*!' And then walk away." He gives her a sideways half smile and laughs.

Apparently ignoring both his arm and his comment, Ashley continues, "And then maybe that's why here I get so—I withdraw so much. Because there isn't that sense of, like, I'm on top of the world here, 'cause I mean you really have to get to *know* me, and it's not just my title or my name."

She pauses. "I've learned a lot in this little talk here," she adds, quietly.

A Leaf Named Tim

"We have to destroy this leaf named Tim," I hear as I walk by Zoë, Gwynn, and Michelle at recess. Gwynn throws the leaf up in the air, and the three girls laugh as it floats down to the ground.

"I don't like this game," I scold. "You would not want people to talk about you in such a mean way. You might not want to come to school."

"It's just a leaf," Gwynn says to defend herself.

"I don't buy that," I say. "Timmy is trying very hard not to laugh at Zoë when she screams. You're not being nice to him."

I decide to drop it there, but to keep my eyes open to see if this is part of a pattern or just an isolated event.

The next day we are getting ready for gym when Timmy, usually happy during every school activity, starts to cry. "I don't want to go to gym," he says between sobs.

"If you can tell us about your sadness, we'll try to help you," I say.

"Everybody looks at me," he says. "That makes me feel sad. They all look at me and I was dumb."

"So you felt like you couldn't do something very well in gym and people were looking at you?"

"I want my mom," he answers.

"What could we do to help you feel better?" I ask.

"Say sorry?" Timmy asks, trying to figure out the correct answer.

"I could help him, 'cause I'm really good at basketball," Russell offers. "I've been doing it in my summer camp."

"If he wants to play soccer, me and Toby could help him, 'cause we're on the soccer team," Sean says.

"If he needs help with baseball, I can help him," Russell says.

"Timmy can just say, 'please stop,' if they laugh at him," Nell suggests.

"We could say, 'Timmy, I don't mean to scare you, but you made a mistake,'" Zoë suggests.

"If he needs help doing ballet, I could do it," Michelle says.

"If he feels hurt about someone calling him a name, he could say, 'I don't like that,'" Gwynn says.

I notice that my three leaf throwers have now offered assistance. "So, Timmy," I say, "if you're worried in gym, you can ask someone to teach you, you could tell someone to stop looking at you, or if that doesn't work, you can always tell the teacher. Do you have any other ideas?"

"I want my mom," he answers.

"One day I was throwing up and I wanted my mom quickly, but I had to wait," Toby cautions him.

"Now that we know Timmy is worried about this, let's all be careful to help him and not make him feel bad," I summarize.

I wonder if Timmy is picking up subtle cues that the children are putting him down. He is still often off the subject in discussions and he might not grasp the rules of a game in gym. Without understanding their comments, he may realize that he is being mocked but be unable to tell them to stop.

Timmy embodies a certain babyishness that is not tolerated in public by the five-year-olds. He wets his pants, misunderstands conversations, and does not play games by the rules; all behaviors the fives still sometimes engage in but would prefer to hide.

Zoë is becoming a more confident member of the group, but it seems there is no end to the pattern of the exclusion of the weakest.

At the gym, I take the teacher aside and tell him what has happened. "Timmy says he feels dumb in gym," I say, "and that the other children look at him."

"It's the game called 'Running Colors,'" he says. "He runs across the gym at every color I call, instead of waiting until I name a color he's wearing. The other kids don't like it." He thinks a moment. "I'll give him a thumbs-up sign when it's his turn to run," he decides.

"The other kids have promised to help him," I say. "But let me know how it goes."

Timmy runs to me after gym. "We played Running Colors," he says. "I got thumbs-up!"

17
....
Give-and-take

At home, I look up *tease* in my dictionary. "To annoy persistently, especially by goading, coaxing, or tantalizing."

I call my brother. "Peter," I say, "How did you come to stop teasing?"

There is a long pause. "But I haven't."

"You don't still make me furious," I say.

"But I still tease." There is an uncomfortable silence. "I try not to," he says. "I like to tease people who tease back. And I use it in my mediation."

The conversation feels awkward, as though perhaps something is being left out.

"Teasing has two parts," he tells me. "One part is pushing and one part is humor. One way to tease is to push people to see something about themselves. In mediation, when two people are angry, if you can tease them and they can accept it, you can transform the situation. I might say, 'You guys have really gotten good at being able to needle each other! It's amazing!' Something where they can recognize, on one hand, what they're doing, and at the same time there's something a little funny.

"But I learned early," he continues, "that it's easy to make a mistake. What one person sees as funny, the other one feels stung by. You have to pay attention to both people in the audience to do it without hurting. The proportion of fun to pushing has to be heavy on the fun. And both people have to be ready to receive it."

"That sounds like quite a challenge," I say. I had no idea his teasing was so complex.

"Sometimes I've gone wrong," he answers. "One time, when I was passing out evaluations after each mediation was over, one guy wrote, 'A mediator should keep his stupid jokes to himself.' So, a lot of times now," he continues, "I do it in my own mind and decide not to risk it."

"Like what?" I ask, intrigued.

"Here's one," he says. "My wife has some friends, a couple, who run this center. One night, they have Sufi meditation, one night it's a men's group helping guys connect with each other at a deeper level, you know. In my mind, I call it, 'The Center for Pretentious Living.' But I won't mention it to her because she takes it seriously."

He pauses, and I remain quiet, waiting.

"Sometimes it comes out before I can stop it. At my Spanish dance class, there were two women, one really fat and the other really skinny. The teacher said, 'Turn your back,' in Spanish. I didn't understand. 'Don't you know what "back" is?' he asked, using the Spanish word again. He touched the back of the skinny girl. I touched the back of the fat girl and said, 'Then what is this?' "

"What did they do?" I ask, horrified.

There was a long pause and suddenly I knew that it matched the pause in the beginning of our conversation: this is the hurtful, excluding part of teasing that he has tried to keep under control but that still comes out before he can stop it.

"Their Spanish wasn't as good as mine," he says. "I was bantering with the teacher and I'm pretty sure they weren't following it. But I still feel bad about it."

After I'm off the phone, I look up the word *scapegoat* on my computer. I suspect that Peter's joke about the fat girl's back and my class's derogatory remarks about Timmy have a similar origin and I would like to understand it more fully. To my surprise, my search directs me to Leviticus 16:21–23. "And Aaron shall lay both hands upon the head of the live goat, and shall confess all the iniquities of the children of Israel, and all their transgressions in all their sins, putting them upon the head of the goat, and shall send him away by the hand of a fit man into the wilderness. And the goat shall bear upon him all their iniquities unto a land uninhabited; and he shall let go the goat in the wilderness. "

I look up *iniquities, transgressions,* and *sins,* wondering what exactly is the heavy load this goat must carry into the wilderness. *Transgressions,* it seems, refers to infringements of community law; *sins* are offenses against religious or moral law, while *iniquities* involve wickedness against God.

Timmy's babyishness is a transgression in the community of five-year-olds. Noah's vulnerability, his intense wish to belong to the boys' group, is also a weakness that is unacceptable to them. Being fat, in our culture, is another offense, one that my brother might like to send off into the desert. How much easier it would be if all these sins could be carried off into the desert by just one goat.

Monday morning I catch sight of Toby, walking by the sand table, crushing an elaborate tunnel system with his hand as he goes by. "Toby!" I exclaim.

The guilty and hurt look on his face reminds me of Peter telling me of his remark about the fat woman. I believe that Toby, too, is wishing he could take it back.

"Noah, Toby knocked in your sand tunnel," Brooke calls out.

Unexpectedly, I want to protect Toby. "It's clean-up time anyway," I announce quickly.

On the way home, I pick up a copy of *Between Give and Take: A Clinical Guide to Contextual Therapy,* by Ivan Boszormenyi-Nagy. I want to know how I can help the child who feels destructively entitled to find a more constructive way to redress his grievances.

"The more relatively helpless and vulnerable the victim and the more injurious and irreversible the harm suffered," I read, "the more the victim is likely to accumulate destructive entitlement. . . . The destructively entitled person characteristically overlooks the fact that he is not entitled to take out his basically justifiable grudge on innocent others."

If Toby or Zoë is reacting to such a grudge, telling them not to exclude or tease will clearly not solve the problem.

I keep looking. "The most important task," I read, "is to help such a person discover self-rewarding avenues of autonomy and trust building."

I call Peter. "How do I do this?" I ask, reading him the quotes.

"Nagy says there are four levels of thinking about things that happen between people," Peter says. "There are the facts, the interactions, the emotions, and the ethical dimension. He says that the dimension where talking leads to healing is the ethical dimension: who gave, who received, who took from, what was fair or unfair, who took advantage, etc. That's what kids like to talk about with each other, but generally adults don't listen, much less try to further the discussion. But that's what I know you like to talk about with your kids."

"Like 'If she came here everyone would play with her,' or 'Someone who wasn't my friend was taking away all my friends'?" I ask, remembering Zoë's bad day.

"That's right," he says. "I wish I could have had discussions like that when I was in elementary school. I felt like I was all alone, trying to come to grips with issues like being left out and being bullied."

You, left out and bullied? You were the popular one, the star of the basketball team, the straight A student. Listening to Peter's view, I begin to give up old resentments and become more curious, less judgmental.

I've learned a lot in this little talk here, I tell myself, remembering Ashley's comment at the end of our discussion. If this conversation can help me to change from being critical to becoming curious, what might our group discussions do for the children?

18

....

It's All about Me

I am puzzled by the need of my three older girls, Zoë, Gwynn, and Ariel, to be so mean to Timmy, who seems to pose such a small threat to them. During April vacation, I decide to ask Ashley her opinion. It will give me an opportunity to find out what she's been doing since we talked last.

She meets me alone this time, at a coffee shop near her school, and we sit at a small table, eating muffins and drinking coffee. Her hair streaks are green and now she has earrings all the way up the rim of her ear.

"I mean, I did that with Dylan," Ashley says when I tell her that I am concerned about Timmy being ostracized by the older girls in my class. "He was my boyfriend last year and we had this really awkward relationship. And this year, when we came back to school, he asked me out again. When he first asked me out, last year, I convinced him that I really didn't want anything to do with him. I convinced the entire school that I hated him. I was like, 'Why am I so adamant about not being with him?' And it was, like, he was not up to my standards of excellence; he was not appealing to me, and then I was like, 'There are better things than that,' and like 'That doesn't really matter.' And we started going out. And we joke about it, 'cause after I said, 'OK, I'll be your girlfriend,' I said, 'But we have to get some things straight,' and he was like, 'What?' and I was like, 'Oh. One: It's all about me. And two: It's always on my terms.' And boy, I was really mean to him, and my friends were like, 'I can't believe you said that!' And like afterward, there was this point where it got so bad that I felt physically sick. And I wrote him this letter about how sorry I was, and I was, like, crying and stuff. And I gave it to him and he like thanked me, you know. And then when he asked me out this year, I avoided him for three days, so it was like this humility thing, where it's not about pride, it's about you like him. And I've liked him for two years, but he's not the type of guy I've normally gone out with, I guess. Like the type of guy I've normally gone out with is like the really hot guy that's, like, friends with everyone and is really funny but is a really big asshole. And he's not like that at all. I don't know; I'm still struggling with it. He's like, 'We need to talk about this all-on-your-terms thing,' and I've been avoiding it, but I know he really does want to talk about it."

"Do you think you will?" I ask.

"I think I will," she answers, "but I'll kind of joke about it, because now a bunch of people call me 'princess' and stuff. I made it into a joke, so I don't have to deal with it, 'cause I know it's a problem, I know it's not the right thing, I know it's bad. But I just don't know, I don't like thinking about it, 'cause if one of my friends was doing it, I'd probably say, 'You're insecure—you're just trying to fill a void.' That's probably what I'd say to someone who was doing it. And *I'm* doing it!

"We got in a big fight yesterday," she continues. "He said he was nervous, or something. And I took it the wrong way, I guess, like, meaning 'I don't want to be with you.' So, I flipped out and I wouldn't let him talk and I said, 'I don't want to talk to you about it.' And he said, 'Why?' and I said, 'Because I don't get hurt.' And I was like, 'I don't get hurt and I don't get mad and I don't get upset. So, we're not gonna talk about this.' And he said, 'Why?' And I said, ''Cause it's always on my terms,' and I walked out and I went back to my room and I, like, bawled for two hours, like uncontrollably. And then my friend was like, 'He's scared to come talk to you,' and I was like, 'Oh, no!'

I asked her, 'Why?' and she said, 'Because you're so unpredictable, sometimes. You let your emotions drag you everywhere.' So, I was like, 'Oh.'

"So, I went and I talked to him and I was like, 'You have to understand. I do that because I don't like being vulnerable. And I always have to have the last word because I want to feel like it's gonna work out for me, and I'm not gonna be hurt.' And I told him I was really upset and crying and he felt bad. But I told him I felt worse. But he knows I'm struggling with this. And I've talked with him about things that happened to me with other relationships, 'cause I have a huge trust issue, which is probably where most of this comes from. And, um . . ."

Ashley plays with a muffin crumb on the table, while I wonder if I should interrupt her unusual silence.

"Because I was raped four times," she continues, "and so I haven't really . . . I've talked a little bit about it with a shrink, but I didn't really talk about it that much. And she kept wanting to relate everything, like all my problems, back to the fact that I was adopted. So, that really didn't work out. And after that, it was like, I'm not going to talk about it with anyone. But it definitely shows. Like, people pick up on it. And it was like Dylan said, 'I know you have trust issues, but how can I deal with your whole power tripping, and all that stuff?' "

I think of Zoë, also vulnerable and in need of protection. She does not believe the group will provide that safe haven. Instead, her rich fantasy life helps her feel safe:

"There's a mommy unicorn and she's laying down with the dad unicorn. The two boys and two girls are watching. The mom tells them all a story. Two Minotaurs come along and they try to eat the newborn that's laying right on the mom's tummy and the baby screams about Minotaurs. And then the dad kicks the Minotaur and the Minotaur runs away."

To Zoë, the group is dangerous and cannot be counted on for safety. But for Ashley, the opposite is true: she feels safer in the group than alone.

"It makes sense," I tell Ashley, "that you want to have a strong group to protect you."

"I always feel like I need to have someone there to protect me," she says. "And I don't want to say that, because I don't want to be, like, 'I need help,' so the fact that I can be a part of a group just takes care of that. Then I don't have to worry."

19

. . . .

Under Their Wings

Thinking of the strategy Ashley mentioned in our first meeting, I wonder if I can find a girl who can take Zoë under her wing. I arrange a small lunch table for Zoë, Gwynn, and Nell. If anyone can protect and teach Zoë, it will be these two: They are liked by everyone, both boys and girls. They love the same kind of fantasy play that Zoë enjoys, and they are both flexible enough to be able to change their game to incorporate another child.

Yet each day, when Zoë goes to get her lunch box and wash her hands, she gets upset before she has even arrived at her table. She shouts that she doesn't like the food in her lunch box or that Noah's backpack is in her way or that she hates washing her hands because the paper towels smell bad. By the time she gets to her table, she is too upset to gain much from the experience, and Nell and Gwynn feel awkward and uncomfortable with her fussing. They like play and conversation to go smoothly and they prefer to avoid such outbursts.

To see if I can head off this daily problem, I sit down by Zoë when she is at recess, collecting small stones in the pine grove.

"I noticed you get upset when you get ready for lunch," I say.

"That's because I hate it that Nell and Gwynn sit down first and they're having such a good time eating lunch without me!" she exclaims.

I had no idea that was bothering her and I wish that I had asked sooner.

"What could we do about that?" I ask her.

"I could get ready for lunch quicker," she says.

"I know you don't like to wash your hands in the bathroom," I say, "so maybe you could wash up at the big teacher's sink near the art table." Hand washing, I know, is a problem to her. She doesn't like the smell of our soap or paper towels and it takes her a while to get the job done to her satisfaction. I have been reluctant to let the children use the art area sink for hand washing because they quickly use up the entire roll of towels, leaving me unable to mop up the inevitable paint spills.

"If you want," I tell her, "we could talk about the lunch problem with Nell and Gwynn."

"OK," Zoë says.

I sit down with the three girls before lunch. "Zoë told me that she feels left out when you start eating your lunch without her," I tell Gwynn and Nell. "Sometimes it takes her a longer time to wash up."

"Oh! We'll wait for her!" Gwynn says cheerfully. They get their lunch boxes, and they wait while Zoë rinses and wipes her hands and checks to make sure they smell good. When she sits down, they all begin to eat.

20

....

Caboose

Toby's wish to be first in line had been so intense that he knocked over chairs and crashed into children as he sprinted to the door when we got ready to go to gym or recess. Long arguments about who got there first ensued, making the gym teacher annoyed with our lateness to class. In frustration and to protect everyone's safety, I had decided the children would line up in alphabetical order, taking turns to be the leader.

But now, as we line up for recess, it is Zoë's turn to be last. "I don't want to be the caboose!" she wails, refusing to get ready to go.

"Zoë," I tell her. "We'll try to solve this problem, but here's what I want you to do: we'll collect everyone's ideas and you listen to all of them without interrupting. And then you tell us if you think any of them might work, OK?"

This is a bit risky. She could like an idea that's unacceptable to me or to many other children or they might give in to her rather than have to put up with her tantrums. But if we are to help Zoë to become a constructive member of the group, like Kirk in the wilderness, then this is a good place to begin.

"Maybe every time she's last, she can go in front of someone else," Brooke says. "Or ask if someone else would like to go last." Brooke's interpretation of the rules seems to be becoming more flexible.

"Well," Toby says, "they could stand next to the person."

"I could be the caboose with her," Gwynn offers, clarifying Toby's idea.

"You don't mind?" I ask.

"It's OK with me," she says.

"I would like to be the caboose," Caleb says.

"Zoë could, like, go behind the line leader so she could be the door holder." Michelle suggests.

"No, not always," Brooke says. This is going too far for her: Brooke likes to hold the door, the job of the second in line.

"She doesn't have to mind because she's in the back," Michelle says. "She could pretend that somebody's in back of her."

"Well," Zoë says, "what we could do is when it's my turn to be the caboose, there could be two people in the caboose at a time. So, all the time there would be two people at the end of the line."

"So, the person last in line could choose to be partners with the person who's next to the last?" I say.

"Yes!"

"Yes!"

"Does everyone agree?" I ask.

They agree by acclamation. I think the boys from wilderness would like this solution.

Unicorns Can't Climb Trees

"There's no gym today," I announce at lunchtime. "The gym teacher was sick and went home early."

"Unfair, unfair! Unicorns can't climb trees!" Ariel says. Soon there is a chant and "Unfair, unfair! Unicorns can't climb trees!" is repeated with increasing volume, as more children join in the game.

"What does that mean?" I ask Gwynn, who sits across from me, eating a circle around the outside of her Oreo.

"It means that it's unfair but there's nothing you can do about it," she explains.

"Unfair, unfair! Squirrels can't swim!" Russell says, making his small stuffed squirrel dance on top of his lunch box in time to the chant.

"Unfair, unfair! Giraffes can't fly!" Toby adds.

Soon there are variations all around, with children laughing as they try to outdo each other. The tone of the room has changed from irritation to humor, with a much more friendly tone than the common adult warning, "Life isn't fair, you know!"

Zoë's unicorns are working their magic in other ways, too. As the children tell stories the next morning, I am reminded of their influence:

"There's five baby unicorns," Nell dictates to me. "And there was a mom and then there was a dad. And the babies were crawling around the room. And they were going into a cave with their mom and dad and when they were going home, they bumped into two monsters. They froze the monsters with their horns because they were magic."

"Zoë," I say, hiding my concern that she might not like her unicorns being usurped by Nell. "Listen to this story of Nell's. She likes unicorns, too." Zoë comes over to the story table, wearing her favorite costume, a gray furry hood with a unicorn horn at the top. I read Nell's story, and Zoë bends her head so I can scratch behind the horn, between her ears. I take that as her approval.

Brooke has been sitting at the story table, listening and drawing. When it is her turn to tell a story, she continues the unicorn theme:

"There was a fox and two unicorns and a cat. They went to the fox's house. Then there were two people in the house—a boy and a girl. The fox and the unicorns were their pets. And they all went for a walk."

When Zoë tells her story, she explores a new pattern:

"The fairy princess is sneaking up in the middle of the night at Eunice's house and snuck up and woke up the two gold unicorn babies." Zoë jumps up and down in excitement as she tells me. "They snuck up and woke up Eunice and Eunice snuck up and woke up the Snowflake Fairies who snuck up and woke up the centaur and they all go into the garden and pick blueberries and eat them."

Toby is sitting at the table drawing dinosaurs. "Why do you always jump up and down when you tell your stories?" he asks her.

"Because I'm excited," she says.

"It makes me feel bad if I'm not in it," he tells her.

"I think maybe she really can't stop to remember that when she's so excited about a story," I say, pleased that Toby is becoming interested in understanding Zoë and that he is eager to be a character in her story.

"Oh," he answers. "Maybe she could stop if she can."

The children are delighted with her new story form.

Zoë jumps up and down with excitement as we act out the series of unicorn stories. "I guess my unicorn stories are contagious!" she announces.

22

....

Missing Gym Shoes

I knew for a week that something fishy was going on with Michelle's gym shoes. While she was out with the flu, I kept finding the shoes in odd places. First they were in Timmy's cubby. Timmy, though young, likes to put things where they belong, and I couldn't see him putting Michelle's Barbie sneakers next to his blue dump truck shoes. I put the Barbies back where they belonged, but the next day they were on the little step that the smallest children use to reach the sink. Could they have fallen out of her cubby and been moved by the janitor who washed the floor at night?

The day Michelle comes back to school, she can't find her gym shoes. Immediately, I think of the odd movements of the previous week and I check all the cubbies, the floor, everywhere I can imagine they might have fallen. The children all deny having any information about them. By this time, I suspect Zoë, who is still angry with Michelle over an incident at the tire swing a couple of weeks ago. She didn't like the way Michelle had pushed her on the swing.

But how can I catch Zoë? I don't want to put her in the position of lying to cover up her misdemeanor. I just want her to tell me where to find the gym shoes.

I hear Gwynn whisper to a group of girls that someone threw them in the wastebasket. I check the trash, with no success. During gym, I take Gwynn out and we sit down on a couple of chairs in the hall. I figure if I play my cards right, she'll tell me what she knows and then I can tell Zoë and find out where she put them. I am uncomfortable about pressuring Gwynn to tell on her friend, one that I had encouraged her to help, but if I can't find those shoes, I will have to ask Michelle's parents to buy a new pair. That's awkward, since they disappeared while Michelle was out of school.

Gwynn's hands tremble and her face is white. "Timmy threw them in the garbage," she says when I ask her what she knows.

"I don't believe that," I say.

"Well, somebody pulled me out of the bathroom and I don't know what happened."

"Nobody pulled you out of the bathroom," I answer, puzzled at the intensity of her protection of the culprit. "It's very important for you to tell the truth," I tell her. "I want to be able to believe what you say."

"Do you promise you won't be angry at me?" she asks.

I have to think about that. It's possible that I will be angry. But I remember her fear of devils who were kicked out of heaven for wanting to do something bad, and know I must be gentle with her.

"I can't tell you for sure how I will feel," I say, "but I do know I'll be proud of you for telling the truth. I know that's hard to do."

She turns her back toward me, but I've seen she is trying not to cry. "I put them in the wastebasket in the bathroom when Michelle was out sick," she says.

"Why?" I ask, stunned.

"Zoë was angry at Michelle. I knew if I didn't do it, Zoë would be mad at me."

"What do you mean?" I ask. She is unable to explain. Perhaps she means that Zoë would be happy if Gwynn was mean to Michelle because it would prove their friendship was strong, while if Gwynn supported Michelle, it would mean that Gwynn didn't like Zoë.

"What do you think should happen now?" I ask.

"I guess Michelle needs new gym shoes."

"Who should buy them?" I ask, wondering if she will blame Zoë.

"I guess I should."

I tell Gwynn that I will talk with her mother and ask her if Gwynn can earn the money by doing chores at home. I tell her I'm proud of her for telling the truth and I send her back to gym.

After class, she tells Michelle that she'll pay for the new shoes.

Michelle immediately blames Zoë. "She made you do it!" Michelle says, angrily.

"No," Gwynn says. "She didn't."

Michelle, however, continues to blame the incident on Zoë. I, too, when describing what happened to another teacher, make a slip and say Zoë did it. I correct myself immediately, but I know I'm guilty of a false accusation. I want to keep my image of Gwynn as the good girl: kind, caring, and helpful. Instead, I know each of us contains both anger and compassion. When we try to put all the negative characteristics in another person, leaving the rest of us free of this badness, we may temporarily feel cleansed but we cut off the possibility of being known for who we really are. We know that if others see these characteristics in us, we may be the next one sent away, so we may feel we have to hide those parts of ourselves that might cause us to be rejected. I am reminded of Andrew's comment, "If you are excluding people, you're really kind of like excluding yourself from being in, like, a group."

By assuming that Zoë was the guilty one, I, too, am sending off a goat into the wilderness; yet if I admit that Gwynn does not need to be perfect, perhaps I can accept my own imperfections, too.

A Unicorn in a Pokémon Game

"They said I can't play!" Zoë complains as she comes in from recess. It is winter and the children are taking off jackets, mittens, snow pants, and hats. I guide Zoë through the crowded hallway to her coat hook, which I have moved to the far end of the row, where there is extra space and less congestion. If Noah's backpack touches her jacket, Zoë will say that it smells like boys and she hates that smell. I try not to let Zoë be in the hall without a teacher.

"We're just saying that we don't want people to spoil our games with unicorns," Russell answers. "We had two rooms and they're both for Pokémons!"

When the children have hung up their clothes and we gather at the rug, I explain the problem: "If there's a Pokémon game and someone wants to join but wants to be something different, like a unicorn, is it all right to say she can't join? Some people are saying a unicorn would spoil the game, but others are saying that's breaking our rule, 'You can't say you can't play.' "

"It's *like* saying 'you can't play' and it's *not* like saying 'you can't play,' " Toby says. "Because *we* made the game up and we didn't say there's unicorns in it. "

"We said she could be a Pokémon or a girl trainer called Misty," Russell adds. That seems generous to me. Most of the girls are eager to take the role of Misty, an important player in the game.

"There's a Pokémon that's sort of like a unicorn," Brooke suggests, "only it's one that makes fire. It doesn't have one of those things on its head. It's called Ponyta."

"Rapidash is a fire Pokémon and he can do magic," Toby suggests, following Brooke's lead.

"It's not a fire *unicorn*," Noah says, "because unicorns have one horn and that fire Pokémon has three horns."

"Rapidash doesn't have three horns; it only has one," Russell says. "The two other ones are the ears."

"I think that if Zoë wants to play with Sean and Toby and Russell," Nell says, "what she could be is play unicorns with me or Gwynn or Brooke or Michelle." Nell would not spend her time trying to play where she was not welcome.

"Do you know what I think is fair?" Zoë says. "If you add parts into your game when someone says 'Can I play?' and they don't want any of the parts in your game but they still want to play."

"So, a lot of you think it would be fair," I say, "to ask Zoë if she wants to be a Pokémon that looks like a unicorn. But do they have to add parts that are not even from Pokémon?" I don't expect the children to agree with this idea. To my mind, the Pokémon players have been generous and it's now Zoë's turn to compromise.

"Well, that's *more* fair," Zoë answers.

"What parts would they offer you?" I ask.

"If I tell them my stories," she says, "they can see what I like and that works. You *can* add new parts to your game."

"I think that's fair," Brooke says. I had expected Brooke to agree with me that Pokémons live in Pokémon houses and unicorns live somewhere else in the neighborhood. But Toby, I remind myself, is teaching us that in an argument, each side has an important point of view.

"Let's act this problem out," I suggest, hoping to find a way out of the impasse. "Russell, pretend you and Gwynn are playing Pokémon." They come into the middle of the rug.

"Now, Zoë," I direct, "ask if you can play."

"Can I play?" she asks.

"We're playing Pokémon," Gwynn says.

"Well, think about the parts in my stories," Zoë says, "because I really don't want to be a Pokémon."

"Let's stop a minute," I say. "We'll collect some ideas of what can happen next."

"She could be a fairy princess," Toby says, remembering her unicorn stories.

"A unicorn," Nell offers.

"I think she could be half unicorn and half a Pokémon," Michelle says.

"Maybe she could be half fairy princess and half unicorn," Brooke says.

"Half fairy princess, half unicorn, and half Pokémon!" Zoë agrees. "This way, know what? If someone has a problem, some magic fairy dust falls out of my horn and it solves the problem! That's fair, because I have a Pokémon part of me!"

It is more difficult for me than for the children, it seems, to give up my idea that one side of the argument must lose and the other side must win. The wish to go to the adult for justice, rather than to find a compromise, dies hard. I hope that some day I can begin with the question, "How can a unicorn enter a Pokémon game and make it even better?" knowing that Zoë has enriched our group with her fantasies and her ideas.

"Zoë," Sean asks, "which half is Pokémon?"

"Actually, all the parts are mixed together," she says. "Know what? I have really hard hooves and if a bad guy comes, I can just kick him."

"Want to be a transformer?" Sean asks. "He can change into whatever he wants!"

"I can change color in the sunlight," Zoë says.

I think Zoë's magic fairy dust has already fallen on the problem.

24

....

Let Rain Take Care of It

Looking at Brooke at the art table alone, making clothes and homes for her stuffed animals, I wonder about her ability to enjoy life outside of the social group of five-year-old girls. She is pleasant to any child who wants to join her activity, but does not seem to need other children to make her satisfied.

I, too, have often chosen to remain outside a group rather than to risk being a scapegoat or to be forced to deal with the pressure to conform. I find myself wondering whether a lone goat could survive in the desert or whether it was being sent to certain death.

I call my friend Jorie, a naturalist and teacher, and read the passage from Leviticus. "If the person telling that story knew about goats, he would know they could survive in an arid habitat," she reassures me. "The desert would have the woody plants that a goat is able to digest. It would be able to stand up on its hind legs and reach for them or climb on the rocks where other animals could not go. It would not be like sending a lamb out into the wilderness."

"So, they weren't sending the goat out to die?" I ask.

"No," she says, "maybe it was important for the goat to live so the sins could stay outside the community. But I was thinking about that ceremony. When Aaron put his hands against the goat's head it would put its head down and push back hard. Aaron would have needed help from the community to hold that goat."

"I guess it's not so easy, laying on all those transgressions," I tell her.

I am reminded of Nalasa, the teenager who told me she broke out of her group and doesn't care what others think of her. I decide that I'd like to hear more of her point of view, so different from Ashley's, and know how she came to her independence.

We meet in the same coffee shop where I had met Ashley. "I can't remember being excluded from anything when I was little," Nalasa says, as we share a plate of cookies. She is tall and looks strong, a girl in her middle teens who has skin the color of my latte.

"I come from a big family, like I kind of had the support of my brothers and sisters," she says, "and, like, in school, I wasn't excluded in anything, like I was in all the sports and stuff, and in junior high especially I was in, like, that popular group that kind of excluded people, and then when I got older, I felt kind of bad and stuff. Like, it wasn't really what you're s'posed to do. Like, at the time it felt like what you're s'posed to do, but when I got older I just started not being in a group, just started reflecting on myself and seeing who I was; you don't treat people like that."

"How do you become the person who excludes others rather than being excluded?" I ask her. "I teach children who are four and five, and I can see already that some of them are the excluders and some are excluded. I want to learn how to help the ones who are left out to be a part of the group if they want to."

"I think exclusion is kind of taught. I had pressure put on me. When I was young, I was told I had so much potential, like, you can do this, that, the other. And then you feel like you disappointed someone, you didn't live up to their expectations—your parents and teachers. So, I think that young children, like in junior high, they feel disappointed, they feel, like, excluded, so they have to exclude someone else, kind of like to relieve themselves, you know? Because for, like, younger children, third grade and below, I don't think they purposely exclude children; I don't think they know what it is to exclude people, I think they get in their little groups and it's teasing, and, like, the bullies and whatever their little groups are, but I don't think they really understand the dynamics of it?" Many of Nalasa's sentences sound as though they end with question marks, even when they are not actually questions.

"I think a lot of people are afraid to be by themselves. Like, I think it's hard to stand on your own, to stand up for yourself, I think a lot of people need someone, and to have someone, like, for me to have you and you to be only my friend and support me, I have to exclude everyone else, and raise you up and tell you you're part of my group so you won't be with anyone else, you know what I'm saying?

"So, it's like instant rejection or instant acception. Like either-or; there's no in between, you know? And the truth of it, you really have nothing, and that's why you're holding on so hard because you know you have nothing, deep down inside. But I think you'd rather have nothing that looks like something rather than nothing at all."

Could that be how Zoë felt the day Cassie came to visit?

"How is it for you now?" I ask Nalasa. "Do you still prefer not to be in a group?"

"If I walk into a room," she says, "and there were groups divided up like an Asian group, a black group, a Hispanic group, and a white group, I would just kind of stand in the middle, until someone was like, 'Hey!' to me. Like, I don't understand the whole thing of people needing to be with people who are familiar to you or something. I don't know; there's a lot of racial tension in this school. When I first came here, people who didn't know me would come up to me and talk to me in black dialect. That really bothered me. I told them, 'Do I talk to you like that? So, don't speak like that to me!' A lot of people have told me, 'You speak so well. Where do you live?' "

"Do the minority students hang out together pretty much?" I ask her.

"I think they hang out just as much as all of the white kids hang out together. And I don't see why people are so fascinated when they see minorities sitting together. I heard some white students say, 'All the minority students hang out together,' and I definitely don't.

"And there are a lot of people who are mixed in this school and don't even know it or don't announce it. And there are a lot of people in this school not minorities and who say they are. So, I don't know, it's, I think it's really sad. Like, it shows they have a lot of racial confusion. I don't know; it's just really funny here."

"I just heard that there's a big controversy about the most recent census," I tell her. "It was the first census where you could pick more than one race and there were people who felt that if you put yourself down as more than one thing, that it would lower the overall numbers for certain minorities."

"But who's to say what you mostly are?" Nalasa answers quickly. "If you are more than one race, it's just, like, a matter of, like, art. If you take red and blue, it's purple, it's no longer red or blue. Therefore, you mark the box that says purple. Like you can't say, 'Yeah, I'm more of a violet color so I'm red.' I mean, it doesn't work like that. I don't know. I know when I have to fill out those things, I always find them extremely annoying, so I always check 'other.'" Nalasa's statements are more emphatic now.

"I get 'What are you?' from people a lot," she continues. "I mean, like, all the time. Sometimes it's really funny, because people don't know how to ask me. And they're 'Like, what, um, where, um, where are you from,' and I'm like, 'Uh, New York.' And they're like, 'No, where are your parents from?' and I'm like, 'New York.' And then they don't know what to say."

"Of course, you don't help them," I say, and we both laugh.

"No," she answers. "People don't understand. I was talking like this to my friend the other day. We have this joke, 'cause she says she's 25 percent black and, like, I don't think it really breaks up to percentages like that. I don't think you can really predict what percentage of anything you are, if you're a mixed person. Pretty soon, like at least in this country, come another, like, thousand years, unless some Hitler stuff happens again, just about everyone will be mixed with something. And so it won't be an issue.

"My sister is pretty dark but my nieces look more Caucasian than anything, and especially my niece who's two, she's like golden and her hair is blonde and curly and her eyes are blue and people are so amazed when they see her, like, in a grocery store and my sister puts her in a little seat and people will be trying to get a glimpse of her eyes."

"It's interesting how strong the urge is to want to put labels on people," I say. "Your ambiguous color makes people uncomfortable."

"Maybe that's why I do that so much," she says. "I don't know, because most of the time maybe being from a mixed family or being around mixed people, and I, like, live in a city and there are lots of different kinds of people around, like, if I see someone I think I can I guess what they are, but I don't ask, and I don't care. I just carry on a conversation and I think it's more of the way someone carries themselves, no matter what they are or where they're from. But I don't know, I think it would work a lot better if that's how people acted towards everyone."

"That goes along with what you were saying about not wanting to be identified with any particular group here, because of your color or because of your interests or whatever," I say. "You don't like the question 'What are you?' because you want to be Nalasa, not a group member."

"I think that is a lot how I am," she answers. "I think I exclude myself from a lot of things. I don't know, I think I exclude myself from groups, from friendships, from a lot of things, just because of, like, the group things, the exclusion things, the race things, and the legal things. I like to be on the outside of things—and get an outside look from the inside, you know what I mean? Like, be close enough to understand it but not be, like, wrapped up in it. I don't know.

"There was a big problem at school that was ridiculous. It was like the initials of the girls in the group were supposed to stand for 'beautiful, intelligent,' something like that. And they made these rope necklaces. There were five girls but only four were in the group and the fifth one got a necklace, and while she was sleeping they went into her room and cut it off her neck. And, like, that's just ridiculous. That's like some movie or something like that. If you go that far to be a group or to exclude someone, that's a serious problem. I don't think you're an individual. I think you're an extremely weak, narrow-minded, insecure person."

That must be Jaimie. There couldn't be two such incidents. Could the grapevine have exaggerated the incident adding the detail that the girl was asleep when the necklace cutters did their work? Or perhaps Jaimie was reluctant to tell me just how fiercely she had needed to exclude.

"What do you think would make this school better?" I ask.

"In terms of race?" Nalasa asks. "I think more people being educated. Like, I've seen many Hispanics that have very dark skin. And people think they're black, just because they have dark skin. If you want to know stuff about race, go away without asking or else ask people about their race with more tact."

I do want to know about Nalasa's race, but I'm not sure I have enough tact, so I don't ask.

"So, you wouldn't mind answering the question about where you're from if it was asked more tactfully?" I ask. I look at her and think maybe part African American, part Hispanic, part Cuban, or maybe Native American.

"It annoys me," she says, "because I don't see how that information is useful to people. I mean, sometimes I ask people, 'Are you doing a survey? How is this information going to help you in the future?' And if you could give me a good reason for wanting to know, then I would answer."

I don't think I have a good enough answer, so I decide not to risk it. Nalasa continues, "But I think it could help the school if they expanded the racial diversity. Like, I feel now, the people who are here feed into stereotypes, like, you have a lot of Koreans and then you have some black kids who, like, live in public housing and so forth. If they took some white kids who were not so affluent or some black kids who came out of upper-middle-class families and started integrating the school like that, there would be a much better understanding instead of getting people who feed into the stereotypes."

Our time is up, and I'm getting ready to leave. But as I pick up my tape recorder and my jacket, I think of Brian, from the tech crew, and try to imagine what Nalasa would do if anyone picked on her the way the guys on his hall provoke him.

"There's a boy here," I tell her, "who has guys in his hall who are trying to get him to fight. Even his roommate makes trouble for him. What would you do if that happened to you?"

"I would not allow it," she says. "I wouldn't let my roommate do that to me. If you make yourself vulnerable, people will walk all over you. My mother told me not to take anything from anybody but not to overreact to situations, just to say, 'Karma will come back to them.' My gramma would say, 'Throw it on the ground and let rain take care of it.' I think it's, like, my mom is a very independent person so that's made me independent. Children learn more from what their parents do than from what anyone says to them."

I watch Nalasa walk back to the dorm, her brightly colored book bag swinging confidently from her shoulder. Could she really be as independent, as unafraid of what others think, as willing to leave the group and go her own way as she says she is?

Just as Jaimie may have omitted the night stealth of her necklace cutting, reluctant to tell me just how fiercely she had needed to exclude, I am often tempted to leave out my false starts, my dead ends, my mistakes, when I describe my classroom. Although I try to describe my work honestly, I know that half of me wants to show only the teacher I want to be, while the other half finds my mistakes to be the most interesting part of the process and fights to put them back in.

Maybe if I talk with Nalasa one more time, I can find out if she is whistling in the dark.

A couple of weeks later, I call my friend Kate, her teacher, and ask if Nalasa would be willing to take time from her busy final exam schedule to talk with me one more time.

There is a pause on Kate's end of the phone line.

"She's gone," she says.

"Gone?" I ask.

"She got kicked out." Kate tells me. "She got into a fight and decked a girl."

I picture Nalasa saying she wouldn't let anyone treat her the way Brian had been treated and wonder how the girl had provoked her.

"The girl she hit tends to act as though she were Latino even though she was not raised in that culture. The other girls felt she was trying to distinguish herself and gain sympathy by trying to take on an ethnic group she had no right to. According to the girls who saw the fight start, Nalasa had gone into the hall of her dorm to answer the phone wearing only her underwear. The other girl was yelling at Nalasa for breaking a rule about how much clothing you had to wear in the hall." She pauses and I imagine Nalasa deciding the rain isn't going to take care of this one.

"The girls say she told Nalasa that she was too fat to be seen in her underwear," my friend continues. I think of Brian, and I know Nalasa wouldn't take that from anyone. Half of me cheers, while the other half is worried for her. "Can't she come back?" I say. But as I ask, I know the answer: she can only return if she apologizes, admits wrongdoing, promises repentance. Girls are supposed to be peacemakers, not fighters.

This time I think about the scapegoat, carrier of the sins of the community, thriving in the desert. Nalasa, I suspect, would rather flourish outside of the group than feel stifled within it.

25

....

A Perfect Statue

A late winter storm has left a thrillingly deep layer of snow over the playground. We play outdoors much of the afternoon, building snowmen, making angels, and working on large forts. After about an hour, Michelle comes running up to me. "Zoë punched Russell!" she says.

Hitting is rare in this group now and is taken seriously by the children and by me. I hurry, my big boots making deep holes in the snow, to see what has happened.

"I just jumped into this snow fort that the big kids made last recess," Russell explains, "and Zoë punched me."

I look at Zoë for her story. "Sorry," she says. "I wanted to play in there and I thought he would be a bad guy and I didn't want bad guys in my game, that's the thing. So, I pushed him out."

I envision how Zoë's move to keep the potential bad guy out of her house could feel like a punch to the one jumping over the fort wall, and I am glad I heard her story before jumping, myself, into issues of guilt and innocence, crime and punishment.

"Were you a bad guy, Russell?" I ask.

"No," he says. "Toby and Sean and me, we're leprechauns and our mom and dad don't know about it."

"Zoë," I say, "you were afraid Russell was going to be a bad guy, but is there a good guy in your game that he can be?"

"No," Zoë says.

"Who could he be then?" I ask.

"A bad guy," she says.

"The only thing he can be is a bad guy but you don't want him to be one?" I ask, puzzled. "Is that OK?" I ask the group of children standing around the snow fort, listening.

"No!" they answer.

"You know that coyote game?" Zoë says. "When I'm the aunt? That's what we're playing." I don't know it, but the children do.

"I'm the mom," Michelle says.

"I'm the baby coyote," Ariel adds.

"I'm a fourteen-year-old coyote," Gwynn says.

"So, Russell," I say, "is there someone in this game that you'd like to be? Someone who's not bad?"

"No," he says. "I just wanted to go in the fort."

"If you're playing a coyote game and Russell wants to come in the fort and walk around nicely, not being a bad guy, is that OK to do?" I ask.

"Yes," Brooke answers. "But you should ask him if he wants to play."

"And I think we should tell him where he can't go and where he can go. And where he can wander around," Ariel adds.

"We could tell him he could sleep by the stone wall but not climb on it," Michelle says. "Because that's the 'frigerator."

"Let's act this out," I suggest. "Russell, you're outside the fort and Zoë's inside. Now you start coming over the wall." He swings one leg over and stops.

"Zoë," I ask, "Did he look a certain way that made you think he would do something mean?"

"I was just guessing," Zoë says, "because I don't trust him."

"OK," I say. "Now he's getting closer."

"I jump in," Russell says, putting both legs down inside the fort.

"Zoë," I say quickly. "What could you say instead of pushing him, now that you've had time to think about it?"

"I really don't want you in this fort," she tells him.

"Well, I can go in this fort if I want," Russell says. "My brother helped make it!"

"Yes!" Toby agrees.

"YOU ONLY SAY THAT BECAUSE YOU HATE ME AND LOVE RUSSELL TO BITS!" Zoë shouts.

"I love you," Timmy says quietly.

I pause, letting the silence add weight to his words, hoping Zoë won't turn on Timmy next. "Do you remember what you were going to say to Russell?" I ask.

Zoë takes a deep breath. "Russell," she says, "you can actually play the game if only you're not conceited and don't hog the food and aren't a bad guy."

"I'm not playing," Russell says. "I'm just going to walk around and then come out and not squish what they have."

"I know!" Zoë says. "We'll pretend we don't see you! You'd make a perfect statue!"

"Would you like to make a perfect statue?" I ask, trying not to smile.

"He could be a refrigerator," Ariel adds.

"No," Russell says.

"Is it OK if he just walks around the fort and then walks out?" I ask.

"Yes," Zoë concedes, "but he'd make a very good statue."

26

....

The Upper Hand

I haven't seen Ashley for a few months but she begins to talk as soon as we have each settled down at the coffee shop. "It's been, like, really weird," Ashley says. "Because I still have this boyfriend, Dylan, and, like, he and I have this huge miscommunication problem. And, like, he thought I was trying to dump . . . He thought I wanted him to . . . He thought I didn't want to go out with him anymore. And so he dumped me. And he thought that's what I wanted, and I didn't want that at all. I turned, like, the entire school against him."

"How did you do it?" I ask, amazed.

Ashley takes a pen out of her pocket and starts tracing the flowers embossed on her napkin.

"I, like, well, I mean, he didn't do it in the best way possible. But I just used every shred of mean thing that he said and I just turned it against him and, like, told everyone how hurt I was and all this stuff." Her dark eyes meet mine, and she gives me a half smile. "And I just wholly blew him off. And so now, I have to do all these repairs. And I also was really getting worried we wouldn't have a relationship and I wouldn't have a date for the prom, so I actually got a back-up date while I was still dating Dylan. And so when he dumped me, I just called the guy up and I had a date immediately. And when I was talking to Dylan yesterday, he was completely joking, and was like, 'Why don't you just go with your date?' And I was like, 'Yeah, that's what I was planning to do,' and he was like, 'You have a date already?' and it was like . . . 'Yeah.' It was so awkward." She has traced all the flowers on her napkin and begins to add vines to the border.

"But I totally, like, got teachers and even the kitchen staff, I got the entire school to hate him. And it took three days. I was crying every night. But I was crying, for a large part of it, because my pride was so hurt. And I got so defensive, and so every person I would see that I was, like, slightly friends with, or had even talked to once, they just saw the look on my face, 'cause my eyes were all puffy, and they'd be like, 'What's wrong?' and I'd be like, 'You will not believe what happened to me!' And like, 'He is such a jerk for making me feel this way, he's such a loser! Like who dumps me?' And, like, I put on this whole act. I had a dress on every single day since we broke up, and I did my hair every single day, and I did my makeup perfectly. And everyone's like, 'You look like a doll,' and all the faculty are like, 'You look like a princess.' And I'm like, 'I know. And so why is he doing this?' And, like, totally putting on this act."

I am reluctant to believe she is so consciously manipulative and want to give her a way out. "Did you know it was an act?" I ask. "Or were you so caught up in it that you thought it was—"

"No," she interrupts. "I knew it was an act. I totally played everyone. I was just like, 'I'm gonna put on this act because I have to put on the image that I'm not only better than him and all his friends, but that I can handle it.' And I need to act as though I have some dignity and pride left. Because I was really hurt that he had dumped me. And so I just retaliated in full force. And the school was like, 'Wow! She does not care, like one bit!' And I made it seem like 'Oh, I was gonna dump him anyway,' and just like it didn't affect me."

I'm puzzled, but I decide not to point out the possible contradiction between her puffy eyes and her assertion that she does not care one bit.

"When in reality," she continues, "I went to all extreme because it affected me to all extreme. It was, like, horrible. It affected me in my classes. And I really felt like if I didn't do everything that I did, people were gonna look at me like I had been totally dissed, just totally disrespected, and that I just got played. And I was gonna look really bad, and I was so worried about that. And so my first reaction was that my image is destroyed. And so I have to, like, come full force with this new image to redeem myself. It's horrible, because now I know it was this big misunderstanding."

"How did it happen?" I ask, still puzzled about how it all began.

"We had been talking for about an hour," Ashley begins her story again, eager to help me understand it. "I was like, 'I don't feel like you can come talk with me.' And it was like a totally and completely calm conversation. And he's like, 'Well, I don't feel like I can come talk to you about a lot of things, because a lot of it has to do with you.' And I was like, 'Well, if you can't talk to me about me, then that's not good.' And he was like, 'Well,' and I was like, 'If you need a break from this, it's OK,' and I was, like, trying to let him off easy, but still play it pretty safe. 'Cause I wanted to bring it up first, before he did, so that I'd have the upper hand. And he was like, 'No, why do you think that? I want to be with you.' And then two minutes later, he was like, 'I don't think we should be together.' And my head was in a circle. I was like, 'What just happened here?' Like two seconds ago, I had the upper hand."

In this new version, I notice that Ashley is taking more responsibility for the misunderstanding with Dylan.

"But when we talked yesterday," she continues, "he told me, like, his pride was hurt, too, 'cause I brought it up. And he thought I was trying to hint to him that I wanted to break up and he was doing the exact same thing. And afterwards, *he* was trying to actually get people on *his* side. People I didn't even know were like, 'Dylan talked in our math class today.' And I was like, 'Ohhh, no!' And I'd have to think, like, OK, who's in his math class, so who do I have to talk to, to let them know that really it was his fault?

"And to have to go back and, like, admit that I was totally wrong, that's horrible! Because actually, when he dumped me, I had to get revenge. Like, I wanted him to feel not only my pain, but more. So, I collected everything he'd ever given me and I put it in a bag. And then I remembered I had two Hawaiian leis that he had gotten me during vacation and they were hanging up on my wall and they were all dried up, you know, and I wrote this note saying, 'Take an example from these flowers and drop dead.' And I left it on his bed. And it really hurt him, but I didn't even think. I thought it was kind of stupid, like, I couldn't think of anything better to say than that. And everyone else reacted really strongly. And, like, part of me didn't understand. I was like, 'Don't you know that the reason I was reacting like that and wrote that note wasn't because I was serious but because I was hurt?' And I was like, 'Anyone in their right mind should know that!' But it wasn't that apparent to him or a lot of other people. And it was not good."

"What are you going to do?" I ask.

"Well," she answers, "I started to repair it yesterday when we had this senior meeting. I was really starting to feel like I should talk to him, but I didn't think that he wanted to. So, I almost started crying in the meeting, which is really embarrassing for me. And I just said, 'I did something that I'm really not proud of. I wrote this note telling Dylan to drop dead and I regret that.' And I turned to him and I was like, 'But you hurt me.'

"And it was kind of like my last attempt to salvage some pride, even though I was trying really hard to at least get across that maybe I was feeling some guilt about it? And so last night I was talking to a teacher who was on duty sitting at his desk and Dylan walked by and he had this horribly, like, mean face on. And I was like, man, what do I do? And he was about to pass me. And I go, 'Hey!' and he like stops. And I was like 'Are you ever gonna talk to me again?' And he was trying so hard to maintain this mean, angry stare. And then all of a sudden, he just starts smiling and laughing, 'cause he knows me really well. And he, like, grabbed my hand and took me outside and we just both started laughing. And it was, like, I felt so much better about the whole thing.

"But now I have to go repair this image that I made of me being strong. And I meant that I was wrong. And I don't even know how to do this. And in my mind, I think, I'm just going to play it really safe and I'll tell people gradually and start out with my close friends and then the rest will follow. Or something.

"I still, like, struggle with things. Obviously, I have a lot of insecurities. But I ultimately am a lot more aware of what I'm doing. Like this whole thing with Dylan. I was completely aware of what I was doing, 'cause my image was not going to be shattered by some boy. And I thought it out."

She looks uncomfortable. "But then you felt bad?" I ask.

"Yeah," she answers. "He had me fooled, too. Like I had him fooled. But I really believed that he hated me and that he was gonna, like, try to do everything to make my life miserable. And it started by dumping me."

As she describes her new understanding of the way her defensiveness backfired, I wonder whether this knowledge will affect her relationship with the punk group she uses to protect herself.

"I believe there's a point," I tell her, "when a person wants to change but isn't quite there yet. And that's the most difficult and painful part of changing. You can see you're doing the old thing again but you can't quite stop it. I think the first step is to see it after you've done it. And the next step is to see it while you're doing it. Then eventually you see it a little bit before you do it, and you can actually stop yourself from doing it. You'll get there, but it takes time. That's my experience—it's a slow process."

"I don't know," she answers. "I just think I'm not anywhere near, like, where I want to be. But I'm getting there. And, like, I'm committed to trying to be more aware of myself. Stuff like that."

Stuff That Roars

"The boys are roaring at me!" Zoë's shrill voice startles me, as the children gather at the door on their way in from recess.

"We are not!" the boys exclaim.

Although Zoë has been afraid of roaring since September, she screams much less now than she did in the fall. "Well, I think *maybe* they are roaring at me, but maybe some of them didn't do it. Maybe they did."

"Well, Toby really meant to do it to Sean, I think," Gwynn, who has become Zoë's best friend, explains.

"And I want it to be at me," Sean adds.

"We need to find a way that Sean and Toby can play their game and Zoë doesn't feel roared at," I tell them, as the children gather at the rug. As I say this, I notice my own change in attitude. In the fall I had asked, "Is this fair? Is it following our rule, 'You can't say you can't play'?" Now, in spring, I expect the group to find a solution that will include those who like roaring and those who do not.

Brooke understands what I am looking for. "They have to tell her before they roar so that she knows that it's not gonna be at her. Or if they don't like to tell her, then they won't look at her, and Zoë will know they're not roaring at her."

"Well," Zoë says, "what I think people should do is, like, the boys should roar when I'm sick or at home."

"We don't like that we can't roar all day," Sean says. "'Cause Zoë's here every day, unless she's sick."

"They really want to be able to roar when you're here," I explain to Zoë, "without making you worried about it." At least that's what I want.

"No, they can't do that. That's impossible. That's impossible!" she says, firmly and dramatically.

"What about Brooke's idea," I persist, "that they face the person they're roaring at, so you know it's not at you?"

"That's still impossible!" Zoë says.

"Well," Sean says, "it's not impossible for us to roar at Zoë if she's on the hill and we're down by the slide. Then she won't hear it."

"We have to come up with a solution," I say again. I am determined not to give up, even though the two sides seem far apart. And I am also determined that the resolution needs to include both points of view so no one feels excluded.

"I have another idea," Zoë says. "Well, I added something to my old idea. That they ask my permission if they want to do it when I'm here at school—or they can do it after school or when I'm sick at home."

"I think if it looks like they're facing her," Ariel suggests, "she could just say, 'Please stop! Are you gonna roar at me?' and they'd say, 'No, I'm going to look over there. I'm going to roar at that person that's in back or front or beside.'"

"Zoë," I ask, "are you playing the same game as Sean and Russell and Toby?"

"Yeah," she answers. This is an important piece of information I almost overlooked. If she wants to play with them, she will look for a solution that allows her to join rather than to be separate.

Is it fair of me to insist that they change their game just for her? I know many teachers would say I was allowing her to manipulate them, to spoil their game. I have come to see these children through a different lens. I believe it is our responsibility to walk with her, to go to her level to help her.

"We can roar," Russell suggests, "but if we tell her we're gonna roar at her, she can tell us, 'Can you please not roar at me?' or 'You can.' "

"Do you ever want to be roared at, Zoë?" I ask.

"No, never."

"Then we *don't* ask her, and she knows that we're not roaring at her," Russell completes his line of reasoning. I wish Zoë could know that, but although she's made great progress, this would be hard to imagine.

"Why is she scared of roaring?" Toby asks. Once her major adversary, Toby has been playing with Ariel and Zoë recently, building homes for their small bears.

"'Cause it makes me feel like there's a monster behind me, and I don't like monsters," she explains.

"Well," Russell says, "why can't we do it in front of her? 'Cause then she's looking at us and she knows it's not a monster."

"What's the roaring for?" I ask, following Toby's lead. "Who are you pretending to be?"

"We're being dragons and stuff that roars," Russell explains.

I could wonder if they are "stuff that roars" because they know it frightens her. Or I could ask why she wants to join, knowing the nature of the game. But I've given up placing blame, so I ignore those passing thoughts.

"Is there a way they could roar, Zoë," I persist, "that wouldn't scare you?"

"Well," she says, "if they went, like, down, down, down to the bottom of the slide, then I probably wouldn't hear it."

"She could cover her ears," Brooke suggests.

"No," Zoë answers. "It wouldn't work. Because know why? I know they're roaring at me, 'cause I just feel that."

"No one roared at her!" Toby exclaims. "But when we do roar, someone can talk to her loud, so she can't hear it."

"They could just, know what they could do?" Zoë says. "They could just go somewhere I couldn't see them and then just roar loudly so I heard. But I would know they were hiding and I wouldn't be scared 'cause I wouldn't feel chased."

I am puzzled by this plan, but I am glad that Zoë can imagine that she can hear a roar and still feel safe.

"That would be OK! Right, Sean?" Russell agrees, apparently understanding better than I do.

"Uh huh! Uh huh!" Sean says.

"We agree with that!" Toby adds.

"Are you a unicorn?" I ask Zoë, knowing it's one of her favorite roles.

"She's a mom cat and I'm a kitten," Ariel answers for her.

"I have a better, a different idea," Zoë says excitedly. "It's that whenever they roar with their face toward my face, I'll pretend to scratch them! So, I'll be pretending to defend myself!"

"So you don't touch them?" I ask.

"Like this." Zoë demonstrates a cat scratching, but with her hands out of range of Russell's face. "Yeeeaoow!" she yells.

"I'm a little bit worried about those fingernails," I tell Zoë. "Do you have long fingernails?"

"No," she says, inspecting them carefully.

"She never touched me," Russell agrees.

"OK," I say. "We'll try this next recess."

I begin to imagine other problems that might happen, but I remind myself that if they do, we'll return to our discussion and come up with a new solution. For Zoë to imagine she could join these roaring dragons is an opportunity I cannot refuse.

28
....

The Haircut

I stare at Timmy as he walks into school on Monday. His straight blond hair is about a quarter of an inch long all over his head, making his scalp visible and his eyes and ears appear very large.

"My mom got this new haircut stuff," he explains. "First she cut it, then my dad did."

Ariel looks at him, giggles, and skips off to the block area to tell Toby and Sean.

"Don't laugh at me," Timmy says quietly. "They're laughing at me," he repeats to me.

"Let's talk about this at our morning meeting," I say.

Later, when the children gather at the rug, I describe the incident. "Timmy's worried you might laugh at his haircut," I explain.

"I won't laugh," Russell says. "It's not something that's gonna stay forever, like your ear!"

"I know it will grow back," Nell agrees.

"I bit my nails," Ariel warns. "They were very short. I just thought they'd grow right back in a jiffy, and when I ate my bacon I kept looking at them, waiting for them to grow. But finally I just forgot about it and finally they grew back. So, just forget about your hair like I forgot about my nails."

"I know," Timmy answers, "but the kids at recess will make fun of it."

"Put a paper bag on your head," Noah advises. "Then they won't see it."

"Then you'll just be funnier," Zoë disagrees. "It wouldn't help. Wear a hat at recess. Then they won't see it."

Timmy agrees to try this plan, but I watch him get ready to go outside without the hat. I think about reminding him, but decide to let him handle it. I see Howard, a five-year-old from another class, point at Timmy and say, "Ha, ha!" I move closer, ready to intervene if needed. "Your hair looks funny," Howard says.

"Don't do that!" Timmy says. "You should be saying that to my mom, not to me! Tell my mom not to give me a haircut like this again!" He turns and walks away.

In my mind, I give him an invisible thumbs up. When did he learn to be so direct?

While the children are eating lunch, I thumb through his notebook of dictated stories. Since I write the stories down exactly as the children tell them, they give me a clear picture of the development of each child's language. In early September, Timmy had been the only actor: "I'm the red Power Ranger. I go in space."

By the end of that first month, he had realized that adding characters made acting out his story more exciting: "I'm a red Power Ranger and I go in space and I go in a cave and see monsters."

By October, he had added a plot with more complex action: "They go to the cave and see a monster and they fight and the Power Rangers win and the monster is dead. And they go into a rocket ship and they count down."

But recently he has had a burst of new story lines that include more detail: "My story is about I drive the fire truck and then the alarm went on and then they slide down the pole and get their coats on and their hats and then they go in the trucks and then they go in the building and then they get their tools and get their axe and crowbars, and then they put out the fire with water." Perhaps Timmy's increasing ability to use language to show us his fantasies has also helped him to be more assertive in his relationships.

The next day, Timmy looks happier as he walks into the room.

At our meeting, I describe his encounter with Howard. "I noticed that he stopped laughing at you after you told him to," I point out.

"It's OK now," Timmy says. "My mom brought the haircut tools back to the store. She says she won't ever do it again."

Nell claps her hands and all the children applaud.

29

....

Chicken Pox

The season for chicken pox has begun and we have a quiet week after spring break while Zoë is out. I enjoy the calm, aware, in her absence, of how intensely I observe her when she is in class, ready to intervene quickly if something goes wrong, but I miss her unicorn stories and her surprising ideas.

She returns the following Monday with her neck and face covered with spots. A casual look tells me that there are no recent spots and all the old ones are scabbed over; she's passed the nurse's requirement for returning to school.

"Do you want to tell the class what it's like to have chicken pox?" I ask her.

"No," she says.

"Is it OK if I tell them about it? I have a book I could read about a boy with chicken pox."

"No."

Zoë is unlikely to change her mind before morning meeting. I am not sure what to do next. I know the children are more likely to say something that will make her self-conscious if we don't discuss it. While I am mulling over the question, Timmy enters the room with his own set of problems. His parents are out of town, leaving him with a baby-sitter. He cannot find his lunch box, which he may have left in the car, but he doesn't remember the name of the person who drove him to school. Several children offer to share their lunches with him, but it does not look like it's going to be a good day.

When we sit down for our meeting, I watch Timmy stare at Zoë's face. If I hadn't already asked Zoë, I might have been able to jump in. But now, there is nothing I can say.

"I don't want anybody to laugh at Zoë," Timmy says, "'cause it's not funny!"

Timmy's on the right subject again.

30

....

Awareness

"Did you see your group during spring break?" I ask Ashley the next time I see her. The program Ashley is in stresses what they call "character development," and I wonder how it is affecting her relationship to her punk group.

"I wasn't gonna see them at all, but I went to one punk show and it was horrible," she says, surprising me with her critical tone. Until now, she had only good things to say about her group.

"Like, I was glad that I went, and I only went with a couple of friends. But it was in a horrible part of town. And, like, this was the first time I had seen my friends all break. And I was like, 'I'll just see them once, whatever.' So, I met them there and, like, I came late, because Nick, my friend that took me, was being such a jerk. I was paying for his ticket and it was twelve dollars, which is a lot for a punk show, and, like, this band came all the way from New York and I really wanted to see them. And he came an hour late. He was, 'We may not get there because I don't know where the club is.' And so I was already annoyed with him. I ditched him and I found my other friends there and it was like old times and we were just having a lot of fun. And then, after the show, my friends were like, 'Let's go smoke a joint,' and I was like, 'You guys can do that; I'm not going.' And Nick was like, 'I'll drive you to the subway,' and the subway was only a block away: he wasn't gonna drive me home. And I was like, 'It's a block away, so I can just walk.' So he left. And my other friends were like, 'We're gonna take the subway, so why don't you just not go alone?'

'Cause it was a dangerous neighborhood and I was like, 'OK.' So, they went to smoke a joint. And after they smoked, they got really hungry so they went to McDonald's and we missed our train. And not only did we miss our train; the whole entire station closed. And so we're stuck in this horrible part of town and we were walking for two hours down this street alone, just the three of us. And I thought we were gonna have to sleep there. I mean, I was, like, really worried. And I was like, 'I'm not walking anymore,' 'cause we had been stopped by these bums and they were, like, asking us for money and stuff like that. So, I was like, 'We're gonna get a taxi.' And we missed three taxis because we were arguing. And then we finally got a taxi back and it was some crazy hour of the morning and I had to call my parents and tell them that I needed them to leave money for the taxi when I came home. And it was just a mess and I didn't hang out with them anymore."

I consider the difference between the behavior of these punk friends and Dylan's commitment to an honest relationship. I decide to approach the subject tangentially.

"Why didn't you want to see your group before the concert?" I ask.

"I didn't want to see them 'cause, I don't know, I feel like I've changed a lot. And, like, I was almost a different person when I was with them. And I didn't want to have to go back and get mentally prepared for it."

"How are you different?" I ask.

"I'm a lot more aware of what I'm doing and why I'm doing it. And why I'm doing things matters more to me now. I have a bigger conscience, so it makes it harder for me to participate in things that they do."

I decide not to ask if she's referring to drugs. "Do you think you'll go back?" I say. "I mean, not to those particular guys that you were fed up with, but to see other people in that group? Or are you done with them?"

"I think this is another reason why I'm having a hard time choosing a college," she answers. "There's a lot of punks in art schools and I think it's inevitable that I'll probably go back. Not to who I was but to where I was. Like to that scene. But I'll be away from the people that I've always known and, like, try to regroup and find people that I respect and they respect me for where I am now as opposed to where I was. There's a couple of kids in my group who knew me before I was a punk, and they'll always respect me. But most of them are younger and they have a lot of growing up to do. And I can't force feed, like, any things that I've learned to them."

If the function of a group is to protect its members, then perhaps it needs to remain static so that the members can count on it to always be the same. When I talked to Ashley in the fall, she was pleased that her group was always the same. But now that she has grown, she feels it constrains her.

"Would that group where you can be your new self necessarily be punk?" I ask.

"Well, actually, I don't know. But I've been, like, really thinking about it. Because I know that, like, I'm not gonna have this environment and this community."

I think of Ashley's attitude when I first met her: "I guess it just doesn't work for me," she had told me then, and I realize how much her attitude toward her program has changed. Now she sees it as protecting rather than restricting her.

She continues. "And, like, sometimes I want to put on a dress and just look nice and stuff like that. And that's what scares me about returning to that scene. Because you can't just overnight just do that. It's very hard to get out. That's what really scares me.

"The other thing is I like the unity that you have with a group, even if it's not all the time. You don't feel so alone all the time. 'Cause most punks are people that have fought alone a lot. And, like, I don't know why this is, but it's a lot more difficult for me to, like, try to relate to people who have never really struggled with anything. Well, I do know why. 'Cause I always have, even if it hasn't made me, like, excluded or included, but I always have. Because, you know, my parents are white and I'm Asian, so it's always been like, 'Where do I belong? Where do I fit in?' 'Cause I think I could go anywhere. And so I think a lot of people in the punk scene, like, struggle with that, to some degree."

"What would a punk group have to be for you now?" I ask.

"Well, basically, new," she says. "'Cause I'm actually really looking forward to being, like, the new one, instead of everyone knowing my past and knowing my history and there's no room for, like, letting go of that and starting fresh. It's all like mending, repairing, moving on. I'm really looking forward to starting over. And having people not know me and my past and, like, letting me control it, to some extent."

"Is there a theme here?" I ask, thinking about how often she's told me she wants to be in control.

"It's horrible," she says. "Every time I, like, think about it or talk to people seriously about what's going on with me, I always feel so . . . not wrong but just bad or something. And then I kind of feel good that I'm at least talking about it, 'cause I don't talk about it with very many people at all. And I talk about it with you and the teacher that I talked with when I had the problem with my friends. Like, I don't know, I would like to one day get it out there and feel like I did when I was talking to the teacher—just standing up and, like, spilling everything. And I talk to him because he's so much like me and he jokes about it. I'm glad to know I'm not the only one that feels this certain way and that feels the need to operate this certain way. It's not that uncommon, I guess."

"I think what's unusual," I tell her, "is your willingness to struggle with it so you can have the kind of life you want to have when you go off to college and not just repeat the things you don't want to repeat."

"It's so weird," she answers. "I want to be my own boss, like, not worry about stupid things anymore. Like, be happy and stuff like that. And then I think about how I handle situations, and I know if I handle situations bad, then that's how I really feel inside. Like, I knew all along that it probably wasn't the best idea to turn the entire school against Dylan. And I was feeling bad the whole time, but I did it anyway because I wanted the upper hand. And I wanted to save my pride.

"But sometimes I wonder if being more aware does anything. Because I was pretty aware of what I was doing. And I don't think I was that aware of exactly how I was feeling. I pretty much knew what I was doing and how it would affect other people, but I didn't take into consideration how it would affect myself and how it was gonna affect my emotions in the future."

"I think you have to be more patient with yourself," I say. "You've been doing these things your whole life and you can't just turn it off all of a sudden. But I do think that being more aware will eventually help you figure out how to do things differently. You tend to be pretty hard on yourself, and say, 'I'm such a bad person,' but you have to give yourself more time."

31
....

Bugs!

I hear giggles in the cubby room early one morning and peek around the corner, looking for mischief. Gwynn, Michelle, and Nell are standing in front of Zoë's cubby, laughing. Following their gaze, I see a pile of huge, rubber bugs under Zoë's coat hook.

"What's up?" I say watching their looks of excitement turn to guilt.

"I was part of this," Gwynn says, after only a brief pause.

"Thank you for being honest, Gwynn," I reassure her, remembering the intensity of her guilt about the missing gym shoes.

"After we scared Zoë," Michelle says, "we were gonna put all the bugs back at the science table."

"I appreciate that," I say. "But why did you want to scare Zoë?"

I wait, but there is no answer. I realize that as much as Zoë needs to learn to control her anger, these three girls need to learn to be direct about theirs.

"Were you upset with Zoë?" I ask.

"I am," Michelle says, "because she was throwing trash around the playground yesterday."

"What kind of trash?" I ask.

"Food," Gwynn says. "We told a teacher and she took all the food out."

"And we don't want to live at school," Michelle adds, "and we don't have to do what she wants us to, right, Gwynn? We just want to be here in the afternoon. We don't want to sleep here."

I begin to see an emerging picture of a game of camping out, which Zoë seems to be presenting as a real possibility. "Zoë's mom and dad wouldn't let her sleep at school," I say. "But you can pretend you're camping if you want to."

"Zoë was bringing the food," Gwynn says.

"It's not a good idea to leave food in the playground," I explain. "It attracts animals. But you can pretend acorns and pine cones are food."

"There could be foxes and coyotes," Nell says.

Zoë comes into the cubby room and heads toward her coat hook to put away her lunch box and backpack. "Clean those things up, please," I say to the three girls. "We'll talk about this in a few minutes."

"Know what's in here?" Zoë says, showing us a small jar with a lid. "It's a little ant! It was in my yard!" She is so excited about her live insect she seems oblivious to the fake ones the girls are quietly moving away from her cubby. "Just look at it! A real ant!"

"Is it your pet ant?" Nell asks, taking a close look at the jar.

"I don't really have a pet ant," Zoë says. "I just found it in my garden and I wanted to bring it in."

"Zoë," Michelle says. "We need to talk about something." Zoë, unscrewing the top of her jar to move some grass to get a better view of her ant, does not answer.

"Zoë," I say, "listen to Michelle. She was upset this morning." Zoë looks up with surprise.

"'Cause you can't bring food outside. There's real animals that will attract the food. And if you bring it out, there'll be dogs, cats, wild cats, wild dogs, coyotes, and lots of other things."

Zoë doesn't answer. "OK, Zoë?" I ask. "Michelle is your friend and she really wants you to stop bringing food outside. Would you do that please?"

"Uh huh," Zoë agrees.

"Zoë, we did it yesterday and we gave the food to the teachers," Nell adds.

I interrupt. "Zoë agreed not to do it anymore and I believe her. You'll keep your agreement, right, Zoë?" I say, hoping to end this part of the discussion before Zoë feels too picked on.

"I said, 'Fine!'" Zoë starts to cry. "I don't think anyone wants to be my friend!"

"I didn't like it when you said it was all my fault when you came to my house and we hid when your dad came to pick you up," Gwynn says.

I want to step in to protect Zoë—I know she will only be able to take this kind of criticism in small chunks, so she doesn't feel abandoned by her friends. But on the other hand, this conversation is also critically important for Michelle, Gwynn, and Nell, who find it hard to be direct about their anger. Helping them stand up to Zoë will, in the long run, help Zoë as well as her three friends. I decide to wait and see what happens.

"Yeah, but that happened a long time ago," Zoë tells her. "And I just don't like when people talk about things that happened a long time ago!"

"Would you agree not to do it again, now that you know she doesn't like it?" I ask.

"Yeah," she says. "No one likes me!" she adds, her voice becoming more shrill.

"I need to tell you something!" Gwynn says.

"Everyone's complaining about me, so no one likes me!" Zoë adds.

"That's not true," I say. "Friends can really like you but wish you would not do something. But Gwynn, what Zoë doesn't like is when you complain about things that happened a long time ago. She wants to hear about them right away." Gwynn nods. "Do you still want to be Zoë's friend?" I ask.

"Of course!" Gwynn says. "I was just mad."

"Would you try to tell her sooner?"

"If she can tell me that she's sorry," Gwynn says.

"Sorry!" Zoë says. "I said that when I was leaving your house."

"Let's play unicorn family," Nell suggests.

"OK," Gwynn agrees, and the four girls walk to the dress-up box, dropping the rubber bugs in the appropriate container on their way.

Under His Wing

Nate was in my class four years ago and he still likes to check in after school to see what's new in my room and to chat with me while his mother goes to library committee meetings. Today he takes a look around and sees Timmy's kangaroo Beanie Baby on the counter.

"Is that Timmy's Beanie Baby?" Nate asks. "I could give it to 'im. 'E's in the after-school program. Maybe 'e didn't know 'e lost it." When Nate was five, it was often hard to understand his speech. Now he still drops his *h*s, but I usually know what he means.

Nate used to lose his tiger, Yellow Jacket, daily, when he was in my class, but it never took him long to realize it was missing. But Timmy is unlikely to notice he is missing an animal. He doesn't seem to have relationships with them or play with the same one for any length of time. His play mostly involves crashing cars and trucks. He often plays alone, because his reluctance to share toys leads other children to give up and play somewhere else.

"I wonder why he doesn't play with his kangaroo the way you played with Yellow Jacket?" I ask Nate.

"'E just plays different things than I did," Nate tells me. "I played blocks a lot and 'ouse. House," he says carefully, working hard on the beginning sound.

"What does he do instead?" I ask. "You see him when you're in the after-school program, don't you?" I know Nate likes to look after the younger boys, playing with them outdoors or comforting them when they're sad.

"Seems if 'e's playin' in blocks 'e'll play a little. But then 'e just wanders around."

"I wonder what would help him?" I ask, thinking out loud.

"It seems like someone has to choose," Nate says, thoughtfully. "When I couldn't talk right, I didn't choose talking, so I wouldn't get better. So, my mom took me to a . . . speech therapist," he says slowly and carefully, working on the *th* sound.

"Did that help you?" I ask.

"Now, it isn't so 'ard, so I choose it more."

"What should Timmy choose, so he'll get better at playing?" I ask, impressed with Nate's awareness of his own problem as well as Timmy's.

"Pretend. It's probably the importantest thing. And sand and blocks."

When he was in my class, even when Nate's speech made it hard for other children to understand him, he was always a good player, knowing intuitively how to keep a game running smoothly. Could he show Timmy how to play?

"Would you help Timmy practice play the way you practice talking?" I ask. "You could come in on the days your mom comes for a meeting in the library. I'm sure his mom would give permission for him to play in the room with you for an hour instead of going to the after-school program."

"Great!" he says.

I arrange for a playtime the following week.

Timmy and Nate come into the room after three o'clock, when the other children have left. I am busy washing paint jars, trying to be unobtrusive.

"What do you want to do today?" Nate asks Timmy.

I was not sure how to tell Nate to begin, so I am relieved to see that he needs no help from me.

"What do you want to be?" Nate restates his question. "What's your favorite animal? Mine's a tiger."

"Mine is a kangaroo," Timmy says. "I have a kangaroo Beanie Baby."

"What do you want to *be*?" Nate asks. Nate knows that it's not what you have that's important in pretend play; it's who you are.

"A kangaroo," Timmy says. "My name's Pouch."

"Where do you sleep?" Nate asks. Now that the characters are cast, Nate begins to set the stage.

"I sleep . . . under the table," Timmy says.

"I sleep on the toy box," Nate tells him.

"I don't know if kangaroos fight," Timmy says, "because the wild ones put their tails down on the ground and then they, like, hit with them. I know because I saw a baby animal show."

"That's very good," Nate approves of Timmy's tentative direction. "They jump up and hit. I'm going to get my key," he adds. "Come on, Pouch."

"Why?"

"I seen somethin'. I forgot to lock the door. It's midnight. I'll lock the back door with this key." He takes a key from my box of hardware store rejects.

"I'll lock this one, too," Timmy repeats Nate's actions.

"How 'bout there was a bad guy?" Nate asks, setting up a potential conflict for the plot.

"Yeah!" Timmy is enthusiastic. "There's a bad guy in our house!"

"It's a robot!" Nate elaborates. "And the eyes look like laser guns! We 'ave two laser guns 'ere, just for protection. You want the rifle or the pistol?"

"The rifle," Timmy says quickly.

"I want the rifle," Nate decides. "You have the pistol."

This impresses me as being unfair, after offering Timmy the choice. I wonder if Timmy will quit now, as he often does when he doesn't get his way.

"I want the bomb gun," Timmy suggests.

"No, there's only two," Nate says. "There's the pistol. You have the pistol laser gun." Now, I predict, Timmy will quit.

Instead, Timmy changes the subject. "But I think I see a bad guy," he says.

"How 'bout three bad guys." Nate expands on the idea. "Hey! You thought you could get away!" he says to the imaginary intruder robot. He turns to Timmy. "How 'bout I escaped. You saw him. You shot him." Nate seems to be more generous, now that he has the weapons under his control.

"I break my guy in half!" Timmy says.

"Breakfast time!" Nate announces, setting play dishes on the table, now that the intruder has been vanquished.

"Pretend the bad guy left us a dirty plate. We had to clean up." Timmy agrees to the new direction of the plot and turns on the pretend water faucet.

Timmy is again willing to follow Nate's direction, and again I find myself surprised by the intensity of his wish to continue this game. Nate, with his occasional bossiness, is providing exactly the balance that Timmy needs. Having been given ample time for good play in his own life, he knows how important it is for Timmy, and he gives in enough so that Timmy is willing to continue without allowing him to have full control. And Timmy is willing to give in, in order to keep the attention of this desirable older playmate.

I decide to look for other ways I can enlist the assistance of older children to help my younger ones with their teasing.

33
....

Good Game, Bad Game

Sam and Alex were in my class three years ago, when they were six. They were cooperative reading partners, they ate lunch together each day, they enjoyed fiercely competitive games of chess. But when they went out to recess, a different dynamic entered their play: Alex often said that Sam called him names, and each day, when they came in from recess, they would complain about one another. I was puzzled by their behavior and never felt satisfied that I had helped them with the problem.

This year, when I see them on the playground, I watch to see if they have changed. They play soccer daily with a large group of the older boys and girls, but they rarely argue about the rules or seem angry with each other.

One day, I see them walking indoors together after recess is over. My children are in gym, so I have a few free minutes and I walk down the hall with Sam and Alex. "Do you still tease each other?" I ask, after the preliminary conversation is over.

"Not as much, not as much," Sam answers quickly. "The only reason I did that was to go along with the other guys."

"Whenever he teases me now," Alex says more slowly, "I don't care. But the first time they ganged up on me, I thought I had nobody else."

"I wasn't really saying it," Sam continues to deny responsibility. "I was just kind of going along. I was just playing a game."

But Alex does not allow his friend to shirk. "You were doing everything to me. You were even spying on me. I told the teacher, then you stopped."

"I just thought, 'It's really hurting him,'" Sam admits. "Now when we tease, it's fun to us."

"I think when you're younger," Alex adds, "when someone is trying to be nice, it feels mean."

Sam agrees. "When you're older, you know what they're saying isn't true."

Several years ago, in a seminar at Tufts University, Barney Brawer described the way some boys throw insults at each other. In his theory of "the worthy opponent," he described boys who look for partners in play who can throw insults back and forth the way tennis players look for opponents who can hit the ball back to them with equal skill. The problem I have noticed since then is that the young boys do not know it is a game and tend to take each insult literally, the way they take almost all conversation. Alex, an only child, had learned the rules of this game later than Sam, who had older brothers to teach him. If I had thought about this theory when Toby called Timmy "eyeball-head," I might have explained the rules of this game to Timmy and helped him decide if he wanted to play it. We could even have helped him think of some silly names to fling back, if he wished.

"Would you come to my class and tell the kids about this?" I ask. "We're having a problem with teasing and you might be able to help. We call it the 'good game, bad game problem.'"

"Sure!" they say.

When I tell my class, they are eager to hear from these big boys. A few days later, Sam and Alex come into our room during our morning meeting. We are sitting around the rug in a circle, and Sam and Alex stand, tall and awkward, across from me. They look so large, next to my little ones. They both wear football shirts and their baseball caps are turned backward. Alex, tall and stocky, stands very still with his hands behind his back. Sam, small and wiry, never stops moving—shifting his weight from foot to foot, or adjusting his cap or shirt. I explain that Sam and Alex used to have a teasing problem when they were younger but they told me that now they don't have one anymore. I thought they might be able to help us.

Ariel explains our problem: "Well, we're going inside and we line up and we slap each other's hands like they do after a soccer game and we say, 'good game' or, 'bad game,' and Toby was saying 'bad game' to people who aren't his friends and 'good game' to people who are his friends, and people didn't like it."

Her description, though accurate, leaves out the intensity of the tears that resulted and the way several children were unable to shrug off the increasingly elaborate insults.

"If one person starts giving a bad game to everybody, then everybody will keep giving bad games back and back and back and it will keep getting into a bigger fight until it never stops!" Zoë adds.

"We want to know how you'd solve the problem," Russell says.

Alex speaks first. "My version is the whole class is your friend. They don't have to be your best, best friend. All you guys want friends, right?"

"Yeah! Yeah!" they answer.

"It doesn't matter if it's, like ... a girl," he continues. "You know, they say boys don't get along with girls, but it's not really true."

"I get along with Sean," Ariel agrees.

"If you don't say something good, don't say anything, 'cause that hurts people's feelings," Sam says. He has picked up a pencil from a nearby table and is tapping his leg with it.

"Well, if they're not your friend and you gave them a good game, they'll probably turn into your friend," Toby points out.

"Me and my other friends used to think Alex was ... big." Sam says. "And I just went along with it, so everyday we made fun of Alex. We spied on him, called him bad names, and he didn't like it. They don't do that anymore, so that's why I don't do it."

"I think the reason why Sam decided," Alex says slowly, "is somewhere in here," he points to Sam's back, "or here," he points to Sam's heart, "he felt he wouldn't have any friends except those other guys if he keeped on doing that. And I knew he really liked me, so I just waited for him to give in."

The room is silent for a moment, and I think about how four years of being in a school that allows both boys and girls to express their feelings has affected these two boys.

"Let's just not do the 'good game, bad game' at all," Toby says.

"How 'bout try it till next Tuesday," Alex suggests.

"If it doesn't work out," Sam adds, "you can call us back."

After this discussion, when anyone says "good game" or "bad game" on the way in from recess, someone says sternly, "No games, remember!" and the offender stops immediately.

34

....

The Necklace

Zoë has been working contentedly at the art table all morning. Shortly before our meeting, I see her take a creation she has made of paper and tape and give it to Sean, who does not look pleased. He whispers to Russell and then throws it in the trash.

I feel as devastated as Zoë looks. "What happened?" I ask.

"I made a necklace for Sean and he threw it away because he doesn't want it. I made it 'cause he was the line leader!"

I think of all Zoë is learning: to make a present for someone she doesn't love, to try to be fair to everyone, to consider the feelings of the other children. "Sean," I ask, "can you explain your position?"

"I just don't want it," Sean says. "'Cause it made Russell sad. And me, too!"

I feel relieved that at least the rejection seems mixed with some admiration for the artwork, since Russell apparently wanted one, too.

"Well, whenever someone's the line leader, I'll make it," Zoë explains.

"It's not that," Russell says. "It's that she's givin' it in front of people. And Zoë herself said you're not allowed to give stuff to people unless no one is looking when you do it."

"We did have that agreement," I say. "But isn't this different because she's planning to give one to the leader each day?"

"Right!" Zoë says. "Whenever someone's the leader, they'll get it."

"Well, maybe when someone's not watching, Zoë could ask Sean if he wanted it," Brooke says. "And then if he wanted it, she could put it in his tub."

"It's not fair," Toby says. "It's six more days till I'll be the line leader and it's nine more days till Russell is."

"She should make a bracelet for him," Timmy suggests. At first I think he's changing the subject, but then I wonder if he means that a necklace may be too feminine for the boys. Perhaps if she had called it a medal, it would have been more acceptable.

"I think Zoë can make for two people at a time, so the line would go faster," Nell suggests.

"I think maybe I should make everyone in the class a different thing with something special about them; something that fits them!" Zoë says.

"Whatever they want!" Brooke adds. This is an important distinction. Giving the recipient some control over the type of gift might elicit a different response from the boys.

"Yeah!" Zoë agrees. "They could ask me to make them anything they want me to make them! Maybe I'll just write a list of things and they can choose!"

The children crowd around, telling Zoë what they want. In the excitement of giving and taking orders, the six-day or nine-day wait seems to be forgotten.

35

......

What's Really Important

"We had senior evals yesterday," Ashley tells me as we settle into our favorite window seat at the coffee shop. This time, the view overlooks a small garden of tulips in bloom, and she immediately begins drawing a border of spring flowers on her napkin. "That's when we vote on how we graduate. And there's, like, different degrees of graduation: there's diploma with honors and that's the highest. That means you've dedicated your life to the process, even after you leave. Then there's diploma, which means you're dedicated to living a life of excellence, and that's your own personal excellence. Then there's certificate. That means you're doing what you need to be doing but you're not sure if after you leave you'll be able to maintain it. And there's document, which is like you failed the character part of it. And, like, we put ourselves where we think we should be. And then our class decides and they vote. And so I put myself at diploma and that's like the second highest, but yesterday it was the highest—they wouldn't let us vote with honors because they said no one in our class is ready for that. So, I put myself at the highest. And, like, most people voted me the highest!"

"Can you see who votes for what?" I ask.

"Yes," she continues. "You just raise your hand. And then, like, four of my class voted me second highest. But some people fail the character part. But I kind of also, like, got a feel for it before I went in there, because I was asking people where they thought I should be and, like, playing it safe."

We laugh together. "Of course, you'd have to do that," I say. "You wouldn't want to put yourself high and then have everyone else come in low."

"Definitely not!" she agrees. "The whole time I was sitting there, I was like, 'Oh, my God! Maybe I should just play it safe and put myself on certificate so that people don't think I'm, like, too high on myself or something.' And then I thought about, like, I've been really trying to work on things and look at things. And I just went like that 'cause that's what I really think I deserve. 'Cause, like, I mess up all the time, but I'm never unwilling to go back and look at it or change it or try to fix something. And that's how I am even on breaks, you know. Like when I did call my parents at whatever crazy hour that time, when I went to the punk show, and tell them that I needed them to leave the money outside, like, I didn't just let it stop there. I talked to them about it and I apologized and told them that it was a bad idea and expressed, like, everything that I had to say about it."

Ashley has chosen the risky path of honesty, intimacy, and growth over the safety of her static punk group in which nothing is allowed to change. Her present school has pushed her toward this path by encouraging her to work out her conflicts rather than to exclude Dylan when he challenges her to grow. When a potential scapegoat is encouraged to stay in the community, rather than to leave it, and when individuals are encouraged to look at the uncomfortable issues rather than avoid them, the community can become stronger and the individuals within it can mature.

"I know you have to work at a relationship," Ashley says. "I just sort of understand more about what's really important."

36

....

Bop, Bop

The end of school is coming near and Zoë is at the story table, coloring unicorns as she waits for her turn to tell a story. Recently, she has been telling stories about penguins, mice, and owls but has not told any chapters of her "Mystery of the Dead Unicorns" story. As she sits thinking about how to begin, I wonder whether to bring this up. On one hand, I don't want to push her to tell a particular story. On the other hand, maybe it's good for her to know that I am thinking about her mystery and want to know what happens next. Besides, I tell myself, learning to tell a good story includes being able to tell the ending.

"Zoë," I say, "I've been wondering what happened to Eunice and the fairy princess. Do you think sometime you'll tell the end of that story?"

"Oh," she says eagerly. "Eunice had magic dust on her hooves and she didn't know it. What was killing the unicorns was this poisonous serpent." She begins so quickly, I suspect that she had already planned this chapter but had forgotten to tell it to me. "And it kept biting them. And then Eunice was running along one day and she was trampling the serpent and the fairy princess said, 'Eunice! You're trampling the serpent!' And the babies jumped onto Eunice's head and screamed because they were scared.

"The centaur comes and says, 'Don't be afraid; your mother is doing something good.'

"The fairy princess says, 'Aha!' and grabs the serpent and cuts it in half."

Zoë thinks a moment. "No," she says. "Make that 'Everyone cuts it in half.' "

I silently appreciate her generosity in sharing this important event.

When we come to the rug to act out the day's stories, Zoë chooses, as usual, to be the fairy princess. It is Ariel's turn to choose next and she decides to be a unicorn baby. Sean sits beside her at the circle. Boys in this group often refuse to be in girls' stories, especially if they think they're about sweet subjects such as kitties having birthday parties. The children will not hear the plot of Zoë's story until we perform it, so all Sean has heard, at this point, is the cast of characters. In this case, the poisonous serpent sounds too good to pass up, so he takes the role. Scott then chooses to be a centaur. Noah, who is next, would probably have said no, just to be safe, but since Sean has approved the story for boys, Noah takes the part of a unicorn baby. Noah would never have considered it if it had been a girl character, but these two babies seem to have no gender. Toby is next, and the only part left is Eunice, the mother unicorn.

"I'll be Eunice," Toby says, realizing it is his only chance for a role. "Can I pretend it's a boy?" he asks Zoë.

I begin to interrupt: Eunice is a female role, mother of two golden unicorn babies, and I jump in quickly to protect the rights of the author.

"But Eunice is a mom, that's the only problem," Zoë says, ignoring my interference.

"I'll be half dad, half mom," Toby suggests. Zoë does not protest.

Eunice dramatically tramples the serpent with magic dust, the fairy princess shouts encouragement, the babies are rescued, and the entire cast slices the serpent in half.

When we go to gym, the door holder, second in line, leans against the heavy door as we pass from the small, preschool space into what we call the "big building." Last week, the children walking by would bop the door holder on the head as they passed, resulting in either laughter or accusations, depending both on the sensitivity of the door holder and on the intensity of the bop. So, we made a rule: before bopping, you must ask the door holder for permission.

Today it is Zoë's turn to hold the door, so I stand nearby, just in case there's trouble. The gym teacher likes the children to arrive at the gym door quietly, in, more or less, a line.

I watch as Toby approaches Zoë. "Can I bop you?" he asks quietly.

She thinks for a moment. "OK," she answers.

He pats her gently on the head. "Bop, bop," he says.

She smiles. "You can bop me," she announces to the children approaching her in line.

I look for evidence of unicorn dust, but all I see is Zoë skipping back to her place in line, her braids swinging behind her.

Epilogue:
Lessons from Spitballs

When my older daughter was nine, my husband's job change led us to move her abruptly from a multiethnic university lab school to a white, suburban public school. Values, dress, and customs were different in our new environment. Sarah joined Girl Scouts to help her make friends, but at the mothers' meetings I would realize I was dressed slightly wrong: I would become aware of an incipient hole in the toe of my sneaker or some unraveling threads at my sleeve. This was a strictly Talbots catalog crowd where my worn flannel shirts did not fit in.

My daughter, too, felt different from her peers. When her Scout troop made Christmas decorations, she turned hers into Hanukkah lights. When they took a trip to McDonald's, Sarah, a vegetarian, asked to bring her own bagel but was told that no one could bring individual food. She tried to dress like the other girls, but still looked a bit out of place.

I knew she was struggling with the social scene, but one day she came home especially upset. She told me that some girls on the bus were taunting her by saying that they didn't believe she had any friends in her old school, and they were throwing spitballs at her. Later in the day, while they were lining up for recess, the same girls were whispering and looking at her, laughing. Sarah responded by pushing the leader of the group.

Rather than listening to her and trying to work on the problem, the teacher had punished Sarah by making her stand in the "bad kids'" circle on the way to recess, where everyone in the school would see her and know she'd done something wrong.

I went to the principal. Like me, she was concerned. But although she promised to keep an eye on the situation, I could see she did not know what to do.

Finally, I asked Sarah how she thought she could solve the problem. She thought for a while and then said, "I think I'll tell them that on Monday and Wednesday they can throw spitballs at me and on Tuesday and Thursday I can throw spitballs at them. On Friday we'll take a break and no one will throw spitballs."

The next week I asked her how it was going. "Oh," she said, as though she had forgotten about the incident. "I guess after I told them my plan, we all forgot about it."

What lessons can we learn from this incident about supporting a child who is being teased or bullied?

Michael Thompson and Catherine O'Neill Grace, in their book with Lawrence J. Cohen *Best Friends, Worst Enemies: Understanding the Social Lives of Children,* write, "Secure attachment gives a child an internal model of the other as available and trustworthy. This creates a sense of the self as deserving of care." At home, at school, and in relation to other adults she knew, Sarah had experienced herself as a person who loved others and who was loved by them in return. This knowledge gave her confidence that she would eventually make friends in her new environment. When I asked her what she thought she could do about her problem, perhaps I reminded her that she had not always been a scapegoat and that she could use her intellect and her social know-how to find a solution of her own. As Kirk said of the people in his wilderness program, "They're not necessarily holding your hand or telling you that it's gonna be all right, but they are there to walk with you." Encouraging Sarah to come up with her own idea was likely to empower her more than if I had given her an answer or found a way to smooth her path.

In Sarah's offbeat spitball solution, she made a statement to the other girls that she did not accept the role of the scapegoat. A group may want to pass their unwanted characteristics to one individual, so that the rest of the members can feel at least temporarily free of those attributes. In my class, the rejected traits were most often babyishness and fear. Although the children all shared those feelings sometimes, they did not want to own up to them. The boys, especially, wanted to distance themselves from those qualities by rejecting the children who embodied them most openly.

Sarah probably exemplified the position of the outsider, the child who was different, a trait that nine-year-old girls want to avoid at all costs. Often the scapegoat finds it difficult to reject the role because the group has labeled her with a trait about which she already feels bad. She does not know that everyone shares the quality that is being rejected in her. By singling Sarah out, the adults made her differences more noticeable and gave permission to the other children to reject her for those traits rather than finding them interesting.

It is difficult to remain reasonable when we feel our children are under attack. Our own experiences of having been rejected combine quickly with a strong impulse to protect our young ones. In my case, although I have been a teacher for many years, I did not take the step I would have advised any other parent in this situation to take—to talk first with the child's teacher. Instead, assuming the teacher would not support me, I went directly to the principal, losing the opportunity to learn from the adult closest to the situation.

Having sat on both sides of the parent-teacher table, I know that as a parent, I have information that the teacher does not know. I know my child's mood at home, when her peers are not around and she can let down her guard. I know how today's situation is similar to or different from the past. And I know what she says to me about the social challenges at school, which may be very different than what she says at school.

As a teacher, I know that I have information about a child that the parent probably does not have. I know how the child behaves around other children—how he or she acts both with a single friend and in a group. I know how this child might be able to change his or her behavior to make acceptance by the group more likely and whether there are any children who could be enlisted to help with this project. And I know how most children this age behave—which problems are common at this stage of development and which ones are unusual.

In order to help solve a social problem, a parent–teacher conference needs to put these two different pieces of knowledge together and make a plan that both the teacher and the parent can support. When this takes place, the parent and teacher are working together to help the child rather than trying to place blame on each other. Often this joint support is enough to help the child through a difficult period.

Today, eleven years later, while fully enjoying social and academic life in college, Sarah still feels pain when she talks about her fourth-grade experience. I believe that with conversation and planning, a community can help prevent these kinds of problems from occurring and can make a plan to address them when they do arise.

Thompson, again in *Best Friends, Worst Enemies,* lists several basic principles for enabling schools to address and prevent social cruelty and the potential for violence. The first, and I believe the most important, is to create a moral school. He quotes Tom Lickona, author of *Educating for Character: How Our Schools Can Teach Respect and Responsibility,* as follows: "A moral school is a school where people spend a lot of time discussing what a moral school is." It is important that the values of the community about issues of teasing, bullying, and exclusion be made explicit and clear, so that everyone knows what behavior is expected of each individual. In addition, as Thompson points out, if we all keep talking about the issues, we will be watchful of how we are treating one another and looking for ways to support the children who need our help.

There are many different ways to approach a moral school. In *You Can't Say You Can't Play,* Vivian Paley spent a year discussing with her kindergarten children whether they should have a rule against exclusion. In the wilderness programs, the small groups with their critically important tasks require the participation of each member. In Kathy Greeley's book, *Why Fly That Way?: Linking Community and Academic Achievement,* she describes a middle school classroom in which the writing and performing of a class play pushed the students to realize the value of every child's participation in the process. These "moral schools" or classrooms can have many different structures. The lengthy process of clarifying the community's standards of what is right and its expectations for how people treat one another cannot be shortchanged and should include as many members of the community as possible.

Change can take place on a big scale or a small one. In my class parents have recently initiated two changes that I believe can have a major impact on the moral tone of the classroom. A group of parents decided to meet monthly to talk about their children and support each other. At each meeting, one or two parents would describe both the strengths and areas of difficulty of their own children and tell the other parents what kind of support they could use. One parent asked for help with child care on a particularly stressful day. A new parent suggested that it might be helpful to her daughter to have other parents invite her child over to play. A single mother talked at her meeting about the difficulty she had finding men that her son could get to know, and the other parents offered to help him connect with their children's fathers.

In a second innovation, a family decided to invite every child in the class, one at a time, to their house to play. This took several months to accomplish, but the child of this family made connections with children she would have been unlikely to notice. She felt comfortable quickly with a wide range of boys and girls, finding common interests with a diverse group of children.

In an environment in which the community is working together on such ethical issues, we can begin to help children to develop the language to talk about their feelings, including difficult emotions that might otherwise be rejected by the group. Rachel

Simmons, in *Odd Girl Out: The Hidden Culture of Aggression in Girls,* writes that most of the silent aggression of girls, the non-verbal gesturing, the ganging up, and the rumor spreading, are "fueled by the lack of face-to-face confrontations. If girls could recognize their anger and upset, the intensity and scope of their reprisals might very well subside." Like Gwynn, Michelle, and Nell leaving a pile of bugs in Zoë's cubby rather than confronting her with her difficult behavior, the girls on Sarah's bus were not able to confront Sarah with what made them uncomfortable about her behavior. They were probably anxious to use her position as an outsider to solidify their own fragile places in the group. In each case, when children are able to be specific about the issues that make them uncomfortable, they no longer find it necessary to reject the kids whose presence brings up those issues.

In *Raising Cain,* Daniel Kindlon and Michael Thompson write that in order to have an alternative to the "culture of cruelty" that occurs when boys receive little encouragement to develop compassion, sensitivity, and warmth, we must "give boys permission to have an internal life, approval for the full range of human emotions, and help in developing an emotional vocabulary so that they may better understand themselves and communicate more effectively with others." In my class, as Toby became more able to accept fear and sadness, he was able to befriend the children who showed those emotions.

Helping the children talk directly about issues of fairness, anger, and other difficult emotions will give them permission to bring up problems as they occur, rather than letting them build up and become larger. By listening to both sides of a specific problem, adults can facilitate solutions that are fair to both sides.

The contextual therapist Ivan Boszormenyi-Nagy, in *Between Give and Take,* calls this discussion the "ethical dimension" of relationships. Nagy says that by being open to questions of fairness and by considering the terms and claims of each participant rather than trying to decide who or what is right or wrong, healing can take place.

Once these important discussions can take place, the community, whether it is a classroom, a school, or another social group, must set up a procedure for dealing with the inevitable problems that will occur once the guiding principles are clarified.

Again, there is no one right way to approach this problem. In my class, the children know that when a child feels he or she has been treated unfairly, we will discuss the problem until we reach a resolution that all the children involved agree is fair. This often means that the children involved in a conflict stop playing until we have found a solution that all participants agree upon. In the wilderness program, every student understood that the work of the group could not be completed until each member of the group had done his part. Although the systems for dealing with problems can be very different from each other, in each one it must be very clear what will happen when a member of the community feels he or she has been treated unfairly. It is critical that the complaint is given a high priority and is dealt with quickly and in a way that the community has decided is fair. The students have an integral part in these discussions and a common language for discussing what has gone wrong.

Since there is no one right way to structure a moral classroom or school, there is no single answer to the question of how to prevent teasing and bullying. Teachers and parents can be reassured that the form need not be perfect. It is the essential, ongoing conversations with adults and with children about what is fair and what is moral that will, over time, help children resist the impulse to tease and bully and will help them have the language and the conviction to resist it when it does occur.

Acknowledgments

I would like to thank:

—Benjamin Coen, age 9, for his wonderful drawings of unicorns on the cover.

—Peter Silverman, for his professional understanding and personal insight about teasing as well as for being a terrific big brother.

—Jorie Hunken, for her total willingness to drop what she is doing to answer questions like, "What would happen to a goat in the wilderness?"

—Still River Writers, for ten years of support and helpful criticism.

—All the students who helped me to understand exclusion, teasing, and bullying.